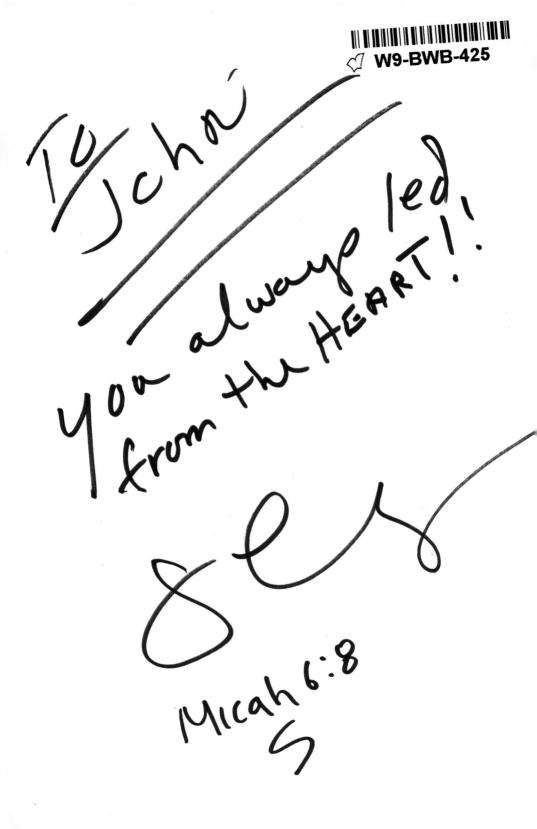

To John

you always led
from the HEART !!

Micah 6:8

LEADERSHIP
AT THE
FRONT LINE

*Lessons Learned About Loving, Leading, and
Legacy from a Warrior and Public Servant*

JAMES L. CAPRA

ISBN: 978-1-4834-1388-4 (sc)
ISBN: 978-1-4834-1389-1 (hc)
ISBN: 978-1-4834-1387-7 (e)

Library of Congress Control Number: 2014911086

Because of the dynamic nature of the Internet, any web addresses or links contained
in this book may have changed since publication and may no longer be valid. The views
expressed in this work are solely those of the author and do not necessarily reflect the
views of the publisher, and the publisher hereby disclaims any responsibility for them.

Any people depicted in stock imagery provided by Thinkstock are models,
and such images are being used for illustrative purposes only.
Certain stock imagery © Thinkstock.

Lulu Publishing Services rev. date: 06/25/2014

For all those who dare greatly in the leadership arena

CONTENTS

Foreword..ix

Acknowledgments xi

Preface...xiii

Chapter 1   An Early Calling and Influence 1

Chapter 2   A Choice to Lead...9

Chapter 3   The Baggage Factor 15

Chapter 4   Doing the Right Thing 23

Chapter 5   Moral Leadership 31

Chapter 6   Throwing a Life Ring instead of an Anvil 41

Chapter 7   Do You Have a Wait Problem?..49

Chapter 8   Stewardship... 61

Chapter 9   Work-Life Balance...69

Chapter 10 The Truth about Failure 77

Chapter 11 What Will Be Your Legacy...85

Endnotes 93

FOREWORD

I
N A WORLD WHERE GREAT leaders are in short supply, books on the subject abound. As DEA's director of training, I was barraged with recommendations for the latest, greatest book that would transform the agency's leaders. Though numerous, most fit into a few categories. There are the "list" books that attempt to simplify human complexities using "150 Most Important Traits of a Leader." Others strike at logic and common sense by insisting that failure is good and that leaders fail because they don't love their people enough or invest in office fitness centers and espresso bars. Some take the opposite approach by recommending a fixed percentage of terminations each year. Each new author searches for an angle or approach that hasn't been discovered, despite thousands of years of trying. Missing are honest discussions of leadership by those with credibility.

Credibility requires experience and success. You have to have "done it" and "done it right." It is amazing how rare this is in today's management library. Books by college professors have academic credibility but lack real-world experience and demonstrable success. Military leaders who write about mission failures and lost battles clearly have experience but by focusing on what *not* to do, fall short of being valuable advice for leadership success. The recent emergence of books by twenty-one-year-old life coaches or children of management gurus satisfy neither credibility requirement. On the front line, theories are separated from reality.

The book you are about to read is refreshingly different. Jim Capra presents an authentic look at real-world leadership. Unlike the other books on the shelf, Capra's successful leader avoids failure, follows his or her heart but rejects passivity, maintains a strong and functional family, and stays committed to his or her spouse. If you are looking to discover a leadership wonder drug that forever alters the body of knowledge, this is not for you. If, however, you are called to lead human beings in difficult tasks and you want to do it successfully, this book is for you.

Jimmy, as he is known by subordinates and colleagues, has led and served others for three decades. From his stint as a young navy corpsman to his current position as DEA's operations chief, he has supervised, managed, inspired, encouraged, and disciplined America's sons and daughters. Through it all, he has maintained a strong marriage and raised six impressive children to lives of service. He has succeeded during tragedies and endured extreme personal sacrifice for the nation he serves and those he leads. Despite his deep personal faith, his strength, humor, and passion make him controversial and irreverent.

In the hours following the 9/11 attacks, on the streets outside a burning Pentagon, I watched Capra step up to fill the leadership vacuum. When nobody knew what to do, he took charge. More than a decade later, I watched as he risked his career by deviating from a preapproved, vetted statement while testifying before Congress. The truth needed to be told, and he told it—and was ready to take the consequences. Serving beside Capra made me a better leader, parent, spouse, and American. I believe his book will do the same for you.

Jeff Sweetin
DEA
Special Agent-in-Charge, Director of Training, Retired

ACKNOWLEDGMENTS

THIS BOOK WOULD NOT HAVE been possible without the love and support of my biggest advocate and fan, my wife, Shelly. For over thirty-four years, she has constantly loved me and sought to bring about the very best in the gifts that have been given to me; she has been and always will be my rock. She is the very definition of Proverbs 31!

I also owe a great debt of gratitude to my good friend and fellow warrior, Jeff Sweetin. Jeff never once doubted that leaders could make a difference in our agency by caring and loving those we were entrusted to lead. Throughout this project, Jeff has continued to take time out of his personal and professional life to encourage me daily as well as read, edit, and provide well-grounded wisdom and guidance.

I am extremely thankful to have been blessed to be the father of six outstanding children, who continue to hold me up in their prayers and have loved me and forgiven me for my shortfalls as a father. My wife and I have watched with great pride as each one entered the leadership arena with love, commitment, and a sense of purpose.

Finally, I am thankful to serve my Lord, the God of second chances, who throughout my journey never forsook or left my family's side, even through some of the darkest hours. I am astounded at how much I have been blessed in my personal and professional life and credit any success that I have to a God who simply loves his children.

—James L. Capra

PREFACE

I HAVE ISSUES—REALLY, I HAVE MAJOR issues with this whole leadership thing. Why? Well, first, there seem to be too many how-to touchy-feely books that come across as simple instruction pamphlets on how to be a great leader. As an example, I have just finished reading an article in the *Harvard Business Review* (you should be impressed) by a college professor and a one-time management expert, touting their three-step process on how to be a great boss. Interestingly enough, throughout the article, much was written about management with very little mention of leadership. The article was a primer for a new management book that the authors were touting. Three ... simple ... steps, and you go from a good boss to a great one ... Really? Could it be that simple?

The bookstores, libraries, and Internet abound with myriads of books on management and leadership written by self-described experts in the field. Over the years, as I sifted through a variety of these, it became apparent that most of the authors came from the field of academia, possessing varying degrees of experience in management, consulting, and/or teaching. In addition, many, if not all of them, have claimed to work at least at one time for a Fortune-500 company, which I have concluded must be a requirement to be deemed credible as a so-called expert on leadership. However, no one has been able to explain to me how anyone can be a self-described expert on leadership or management and yet never have led or managed anyone! My good friend and fellow warrior Jeff Sweetin always warned, "Never trust anyone who doesn't walk with a limp … and teaching what you ain't done is like going back to where you ain't been!"

Drug enforcement agents are a special breed of public servant. We tend to be a very risk-aggressive group of professionals who display an unwavering commitment and passion to serve. Men and women in this profession routinely demonstrate a sense of selflessness and possess an intrinsic need to "make things right." We are, as Lt. Col. Dave Grossman describes, consciously looking for a "righteous fight"[1] to run to the sounds of chaos and the cries for help, to the sound of gunfire. We can't not go toward danger; we are internally driven to it. We define our work as our profession, but, more important, we see our profession as a calling. We live, work, and thrive in a very dangerous and seedy world that the rest of society sometimes refuses to see or does not want to. The decisions made by even the youngest of our agents can be life changing. We operate in a global theater that requires split-second decisions that have immediate consequences of taking life and/or liberty. What is foreign to most individuals outside of our profession is that we excel in this operational environment.

Within our ranks, we have a strong sense of urgency and determined mission accomplishment that permeates our agency's culture, which is driven by outstanding men and women who passionately volunteer to take on the mantle of leadership in this dangerous profession. Among those of us who have been given this opportunity, we recognize the honor and awesome responsibility for the lives of our warriors as well as the safety and welfare of the American public. These public-servant leaders recognize how important the mission is, not just in the pursuit of justice but in terms of the success and future of the next generation of Americans. This is what drives them to succeed regardless of limited resources and often hostile environments. I have often said throughout my three decades as a public servant that private businesses and American corporations could learn much from studying successful public-servant leaders. Yet as public servants, we face a daily barrage of mischaracterizations that are rooted in myths, lies, and false perceptions routinely touted by those timid and ignorant souls who stand outside our arena.

Unfortunately, in book after book, as well as a number of articles, authors and so-called leadership experts routinely point toward public-servant-sector agencies and their relative commands as examples of poor leadership or poorly run organizations. This ongoing assault is routine fodder for numerous keynote speakers during leadership conferences or like events. Very rarely is the name of a government agency or leader ever identified; rather, the offense of poor leadership or poor organizational management is simply and routinely leveled at some unnamed government entity.

Certainly, many of these accusations may stem from the fact that government agencies and their politically appointed leaders have become extensions of the political administration in power at the time. This fact makes them an easy target for those who disagree with appointed leaders based upon their political or ideological position. Case in point was the 2011 "muffin-gate" scandal, whereby the Department of Justice (DOJ) was attacked for weeks in the press for allegedly paying $16.00 per muffin during a conference.[2] The allegations, which were made following a finding by the DOJ Office of Inspector General (OIG), were subsequently found to be erroneous. Regardless, even after the OIG retracted their findings, the media, congressional members, and leadership talking heads were still using this as an excuse to point out the poor leadership within the federal government.

As of this writing, leaders within the public-sector agencies continue to be accused of a number of malpractices to include overcompensation, laziness, incompetence, unaccountability, and mismanagement, as well as a host of other disparaging accusations. However, if these accusations are true, where are the host of government agencies and their leaders that mirror the demise of private companies and their CEOs from the likes of Enron, GM, AIG, Fannie Mae, Freddie Mac, and Lehman Brothers, as well as a number of other mismanaged private businesses? The fact is there is very little evidence to support these allegations. The truth of the matter is that many of the present-day government agencies were created in order to provide a service to the American public, and the employees (public servants) who are routinely attracted to these organizations recognize that they want to be involved in something bigger than themselves, something more important than a large paycheck every week.

After serving for three decades as a public servant and a warrior, I have found that many public servants, regardless of their generational differences, share a common value system, one that is predicated on the notion that they have a duty to serve. It therefore should be no wonder that organizations with employees driven by this intrinsic passion would also spawn and develop outstanding leaders. This is exactly what I have found throughout my years of service with the Drug Enforcement Administration (DEA)—not that there have been no terrible leaders in DEA; in fact, there have been too many, but the same may be true for all organizations. However, the truly exceptional leaders share a common vision and an almost zealot-like passion to make a difference. Although these leaders must operate in a world of endless reams of bureaucratic rules and procedures, complicated by political appointees with varying degrees of organizational knowledge, exceptional leaders recognize that they have a moral obligation to ensure that they remain focused and accomplish their mission all the while developing future leaders for the next generation. Navigating in this political environment without compromising one's leadership integrity takes wisdom, courage, confidence, and common sense.

Yet despite all the above, we rarely see a public-servant law enforcement executive being asked to speak or teach on leadership in the public forum. In fact, it has been my experience that more often than not, leadership organizations have a tendency to question public-servant executives as credible experts, in particular, those of us in the law enforcement field. As an example, during a local "servant leadership" event I attended in Dallas, I was introduced by the so-called leadership guru as "someone who is on a search for servant leadership." When I quickly corrected the individual and explained that I have been teaching leadership and in particular, servant leadership, for years, I was stared at like a chicken looking at a card trick and then subsequently ignored throughout the rest of the afternoon. It was very apparent that although I was a federal law enforcement executive, I was not accepted as a "credible" leader at this particular venue. It was as if the participants looked at me and were thinking, *What does a public servant know of real leadership?* Often, this response is the norm, and the bias may largely be because we often operate in a veiled arena that conjures up a host of misperceptions by many outside of our profession.

The fact is that with over half of my career in leadership positions, I am a "leadership practitioner" not a leadership theoretician, which is the impetus for writing this book. I am not suggesting that the available literature on the field of leadership is not worthy of review. In fact, I will refer in the coming chapters to several outstanding books written by researchers and academics. I am saying that there is no substitute for leadership experience on the front line, in the actual arena. That being said, I believe I have something worthwhile to share with other leaders and managers regarding my leadership journey in public service.

My public service career started in 1977 at the lowest enlisted rank in the United States Navy and has spanned over thirty-four years, more than half of which has been spent in numerous leadership positions. I have served in three military organizations and over twenty-seven years as a special agent with the Drug Enforcement Administration, culminating with an appointment to the rank of the senior executive service by the Honorable John Ashcroft, attorney general of the United States of America.

I do not claim to have all the answers. In fact, I probably know more about what not to do because of my mistakes as well as my own shortcomings and have the wounds to prove that. However, what I do know is what real leadership is about, what it takes to get the best out of your people and what it takes to maintain focus and accountability while striving to pursue excellence in order to accomplish your organization's mission whether you are in the business of public service or for-profit enterprise. There is no magical set of A, B, C's to follow—no step 1, step 2, step 3, and then you are there. Leadership—real, authentic leadership—is a heart thing; it starts with a genuine concern for the development and welfare of your people.

This book is about lessons I learned on my leadership journey as a public servant. While all the stories I describe are true, I have done my best to change the identities of many of those I have written about in order to minimize any negative feelings that may be construed. I am hopeful that in some small way, my experiences will be somewhat entertaining as well as assist others on their leadership journeys. I hope your journey will be as much fun as mine has been.

CHAPTER 1

AN EARLY CALLING AND INFLUENCE

I REMEMBER THAT EVEN AT A very young age, I was drawn to helping others. From my elementary school bus, I remember witnessing an accident scene and wanting to get off to see if I could help. I also recall that during middle school, my aunt and uncle's trailer caught on fire. I ran into our house to grab a small fire extinguisher and then quickly crossed the field, only to be stopped by my dad yelling for me to stay back. I remember how proud I was when I was selected for middle-school safety patrol because, in my mind, I would be the protector. I remember moments throughout high school when I was standing between bullies and other students who were physically and, in some instances, mentally disadvantaged. I thought, *You don't get to bother them, not while I'm here.*

Later, as a navy corpsman, I crawled into the mangled wreckage of a vehicle at an intersection, telling the trapped passenger, "I'm here. Everything is going to be okay." I remember standing in front of my mirror wearing my new police hat and badge, holding a brand-new nightstick, and thinking, *I will make this place safer.* I remember walking across the stage, being handed my badge and credentials as a new DEA special agent and thinking how I was going to change the world. I was now part of something greater. I had been born for that moment and was

1

now in a league with Captain America and all the other good guys who made America so great! This was the call to public service—the call of the warrior—and I couldn't wait to get started.

Every journey has a beginning, and my call to public service and first exposure to leadership started with the influence of my father. Louis Frank Mangiocapra, my father, was one of ten children born to Italian immigrants who settled in New York City. At seventeen, my father left school, joined the army, and went off to war during the Korean conflict. Upon returning home, he married my mother and joined the Port Authority Police Department, and then, after three years, he was hired by the New York City Police Department (NYPD). He would ultimately be assigned to NYPD's elite Motorcycle Division 3, patrolling the New York City highways, before breaking his back and neck in a horrific accident that ended his sixteen-year police career. Following back surgery that fused much of his lower spine, Pop retired and moved the family (a wife and seven kids) to upstate New York where we took up residence in a very rural part of Greene County.

My father, though he has long-since passed, has always been my hero in life. But make no mistake; in our house, Pop was pharaoh. What he said was law; there was no questioning his decrees or decisions. As a matter of fact, I never talked back to my father until my second year in the navy, and even then, I was a little scared. At the same time, my father was a brutally honest and good man. He was not a very big talker; there were no "Cosby" moments in our house. However, he taught me more about character, integrity, and honor than any school, military unit, or academy. He hated being lied to and would tell me that "a liar is worse than a thief!" He would often admonish us to help those who were less fortunate or had been victimized by others. He called it sticking up for the underdogs.

Over the course of my childhood, I heard what seemed like thousands of times, Pop telling us, "No matter what you become, be the very best at what you do. I don't care if you are a doctor or a garbage man; you be the best!" The best in my father's mind had nothing to do with moral superiority. It had to do with commitment, a work ethic, and a man's accountability to his faith, family, profession, and word. "Nothing in this life comes easy," he would say. "You must work hard and sacrifice if you want to get ahead." These were amazing pearls of wisdom coming from a man who possessed a tenth-grade education, if that.

What I most remember about my father while growing up is listening to him and hanging on every word as he told stories about being a police officer. Pop loved being a cop; you could see it in his eyes when he talked about the job. He would often smile, and his face would beam when reminiscing about the years walking a "beat" in Midtown Manhattan. But what became more apparent as I got older was that my father really cared for the people on his beat. He would often say, "I knew everyone on my beat: the shop owners, bar owners, the junkies, the panhandlers, the hookers, the second-story burglars, and they all knew me."

The stories he would tell were nothing like those portrayed on television. Rather, he would talk about people who were hurting, who were surviving, doing their best to scratch out an existence to support their families. Of course, these were interspersed with the occasional story of an arrest of a bad guy or two, but the most meaningful stories were about people on his beat he came to know and care for. Yet, of all the stories my father told, the one that truly painted a picture of my father's feelings toward the people he served had to do with the arrests of local prostitutes on his beat. He would say, "Regardless of what they did or why they sold their bodies to strangers, they were women and deserved to be treated like women, not like trash." And then, my father would look at me and add, "Always, always treat people with dignity and respect, no matter what!"

I learned very early that people matter and that they deserve to be treated with respect and dignity regardless of their position in life, no matter what their position on the economic ladder was. The importance of hard work, personal faith, and commitment, as well as honor, integrity, the dignity and value of human life, and the value of serving others first were all part of a set of beliefs that guided our family's moral compass. These were not just a nice set of ideals; they were truths that would always come screaming to the forefront during challenging leadership decisions and situations. Our family's value system served as a guidepost, directing my decisions and actions throughout my leadership journey.

When I first told my father that I was pursuing a career in federal law enforcement, he looked at me and said, "If you want to be a hero, become a fireman; if you want people to hate and despise you, become a cop!" (Pop never made a distinction between police officers, federal agents, deputies, or anything else; if you wore a badge and a gun, you were a cop!) He would also tell me that I was going to love being a cop. "It's not the bad guys who will give you a hard time," he said. "It's your own agency that will give you freakin' heartburn." He would often say that it was like being married to a good-looking prostitute: "You loved how she looked all dressed up hanging on your arm and how she made you feel. You just hated what she did behind your back!"

It was hard for me to understand what he was trying to tell me because I am sort of a slow learner, but after about a week on the job in New York City, I quickly came to realize that not everybody loved cops or agents (but everybody really did love a fireman!). It took me a little longer to fully appreciate what he meant when he said, "Your own agency will give you freakin' heartburn."

Shortly after I arrived in Los Angeles as a very new special agent, our group went out on a drug bust and arrested a couple of bad guys who had delivered several kilograms of cocaine to an undercover agent. As we began to depart the area, the senior agent on the scene, Danny, ordered me to drive the suspect's car back to the field division. The car's hubcaps were more expensive than the vehicle itself, and I suggested we should just have the vehicle towed to an impound yard. Danny just looked at me sternly and ordered me to get the car back to the DEA office. I complied with his order and parked the vehicle in our parking structure. Then I brought the keys up to our office and dropped them off on the case agent's desk. End of story, I thought, but I was wrong.

One early morning, about two months after this arrest, I was ordered into the group supervisor's office. As soon as I entered the small office, I could see the anger on the supervisor's face. He berated me about not knowing my job and asked how I could ever have let this happen. All the while, Danny stood behind him, looking at me with blatant disgust. While the supervisor continued to yell, I was trying to wrap my mind around what I had done, what mistake I had made. My mind was racing, going over the recent events of the past week, when I latched onto the next thing that came out of the supervisor's mouth: "If I go down for this, I am taking you with me!" *Taking me down with you? I have just over four months on the job, and you want to take me down with you!* My mind continued to race, thinking this was something out of a television movie. I asked myself, *What sinister act did I do?* I didn't steal anything; I didn't kill anyone. The supervisor screamed out, "Now get that car out of our parking structure and get it to the seized custodian!"

"The car? What car? What are you talking about?" I asked.

Then Danny spoke up smugly, "The car I told you to process for seizure."

I thought for a second. "Oh, the car with the fancy hubcaps!" I was absolutely enraged; Danny was a liar and never told me to process anything, just to get the car back to the division. As I walked out of his office, I was incredibly mad, confused, scared, and most of all … how do you process something for seizure?

I would soon learn, thanks to another seasoned agent, that when we took custody of a vehicle, there was a process by which we formally seized the vehicle or released the vehicle back to the owner or lien holder under a very strict time frame. Of course, I had no idea and was never taught this procedure as a new guy; I was just following orders to get the car back to the office. Apparently, Danny, the senior agent, never thought to follow up with the new guy about the car until the parking car attendant gave us a call (two months later) to let us know that the car had been vandalized. After learning about the vehicle, Danny (a self-centered coward), protecting his ass, went into the supervisor and threw the new guy under the bus. Because of my ignorance, we (DEA) would now be responsible for repairing the vehicle prior to releasing it. In addition, the incident was required to be reported up through the chain of command in the event there was ever any civil litigation. It was simply a mistake because of my ignorance, not a criminal violation or penalty worthy of death or any serious discipline, for that matter. I know what I said earlier; I wasn't taught the process, but that's no excuse and I should have at least asked what to do next with the vehicle. But being very green sometimes comes with a level of ignorance for new employees.

The lesson I learned wasn't about Danny. Many organizations have a Danny or two; it was about the supervisor and his reaction and what that cemented in my mind as a young, new DEA employee. The supervisor was fearful that any issue might somehow make him look bad, and at the first sign of trouble, at the first sign of a mistake or an issue, this supervisor would do everything he could to minimize his responsibility and point the finger at his people! I would never fully trust him and would learn that the rest of the agents in the group felt the same way. I began to hear my father's words in my mind: "It's not the bad guys who will give you a hard time; it's your own agency that will give you freakin' heartburn." What Pop was trying to get across was simple; you see, it is quite possible to love your profession, to love your calling, but to hate or despise your organization because of poor leadership, and that can be a recipe for organizational disaster.

CHAPTER 2

A CHOICE TO LEAD

TODAY, THERE ARE UNTOLD NUMBERS of books and seminars on effective leadership. Many of these teach and describe the so-called "competencies" of leaders. According to some, managers are expected to demonstrate a variety of competencies in order to be effective leaders. I have read many a book that described the effective leader as having as many as fifteen competencies. There are even some organizations that utilize questionnaires that list a host of behavioral competencies to measure the effectiveness of a manager. But is this true? Is it effective or even possible? Better yet, what if you fall short of a few competencies? Are you no longer effective? I don't believe that the authors or organizations are necessarily wrong in identifying certain competencies; what I do think they are describing is the "perfect" or "ideal" leader, which is an unreasonable expectation. That is because, as human beings, we all have opinions, faults, and shortcomings that often make us who we are. It doesn't necessarily have to detract from us being an effective leader; it's just a part of who we are.

Being a good manager or a supervisor does not automatically equate to being a good leader. There are very good managers and supervisors who are effective at just that … management. Management, or for that matter, *good* management, should be a strong trait of an effective leader.

Management is nothing more than putting people and resources to work in an efficient way. That being said, retired US Navy Admiral Grace Hopper stated that "you manage *things*—you lead *people*."[3] So it takes more than good managerial or supervisory skills to be an effective and competent leader. All the books in the world, this one included, will not ultimately prepare you to be a good leader. Leadership, especially *effective* leadership, takes doing; it requires one to be in the arena experiencing. It takes making mistakes. It takes courage. It takes pain and sorrow. It takes learning and empathizing and caring and *loving* those who work with you and for you. While everyone has the potential to lead successfully, it is important to understand that leaders *choose* to lead. Ahh, but the question I ask many an audience is "Why?" Why did you make the choice? What was the motive to take the position? In other words, what is your motive to lead?

I was utterly excited about being promoted to a group supervisor, and I had every right to be. I was passionate about my job and even more passionate about my organization. I lived and loved my profession because talented individuals took time out to train and mentor me. There were times I found it difficult to go home at night because of what I might miss or what might occur on the street. I had always believed, and still do, that I was incredibly blessed for having the opportunity to serve the American public as a special agent with the Drug Enforcement Administration. It was now my high honor to supervise men and women of the same kindred spirit. I would love them, and they would love me; together, we would storm the gates of hell to make New Jersey a safer place—or so I thought!

My baptism into the world of supervision was immediate and without warning. I was incredibly naive to what I would later describe as the "baggage factor" when it came to understanding employee behavior and performance. When I reported to the New Jersey Field Division, I quickly found out that I had an employee who routinely did not show up for work. In fact, the employee would call in and advise the secretary that he was on "leave without pay" due to the fact he had no more annual or sick leave. Wanting to be an understanding and attentive boss who refused to believe that this was intentional, I would first gather all my facts. To my surprise, I determined that this employee was a senior employee who at best was a subpar performer. I further determined that his numerous past performance evaluations were all "outstanding" with little or no justification. I soon became intimately familiar with our administrative manual, inspection manual, and our agent's manual, including sections I had no idea existed. (All the while, I am thinking, *No one told me about this part of being a leader!*) After gathering my facts, I was now ready to call in this employee and determine what the underlying problem was.

I began paging Billy the next day starting around 9:30 a.m. and did not receive a reply throughout the entire day. By early that evening, I had lost all sense of rationalization, as I determined that I was purposely being ignored. By late in the day, I was seething with anger and all I could think of was that I now wanted to fight Billy—no kidding, I played over and over in my mind how I would walk up to him and just punch him in his head for ignoring me! (This type of leadership behavior is not found in any leadership book that I know of.) My last-ditch effort to contact Billy was to leave a message on his home voice machine at about 7:00 p.m. that night explaining that I had been trying to contact him all day. At about 10:30 p.m., Billy contacted me on my cell phone. He was unapologetic in his explanation that he never received my pages. In my frustration and anger, I couldn't think straight but was able to order him to be in my office by 9:00 a.m. the next day. I didn't sleep much that night as I went over and over in my mind how I would approach my conversation with Billy. I would be methodical and understanding in my attempt to explain the error of his ways. Surely after my counseling, Billy would have an epiphany and suddenly walk out a more determined and focused employee. In my mind, it sounded good at the time. The following is my exact recollection of my conversation with Billy the next morning.

"Hey, boss, what's up?"

"What's up, Billy? What's up is that I have been here for three weeks and have seen you only once. That's what's up! So, Billy, I figure there has to be only one of three explanations. How are you, Billy? Are you sick?"

"No, boss, I'm fine."

"No really, Billy, you can tell me. Have you been ill? Are you being seen by a doctor?"

"No, boss. Really, I am fine. I'm telling you I am okay ..."

"Well, okay, Billy, then something is wrong here in the group. Is that it?"

"No, boss, no problem."

"Come on, Billy; you have a problem with the guys? Is that it? They don't get along with you? Is this the problem here?"

"Not at all, boss. I love this group; this is a great bunch of guys!"

"Okay, Billy, I see; you're not sick, and you don't have a problem with the group ... *so I guess the real reason is that you think your new supervisor is a $@#%&*! idiot and you are trying to get over on him!*"

Now let me make this perfectly clear: I had not read *Lincoln on Leadership* or any other leadership books at the time of this incident. I do not routinely endorse the use of foul language toward employees and subsequently realized that a manager could actually get days off for using foul language. However, my initial response was effective if for only a limited period of time. Billy's demeanor instantly changed, and he sat straight up in his chair and began to utilize a very respectful tone with "No, sir," and "Yes, sir." He looked like the proverbial deer caught in the headlights. As I calmed myself down, I began to explain what I expected from agents who worked with me, and as I discussed my expectations, it became clear that Billy had never had this type of conversation before with any other supervisor. In fact, I would later find out that since Billy was a senior employee, his previous supervisors had allowed him to operate on his terms and not on the terms of the organization. Having no accountability, Billy had lost all sense of personal and organizational discipline.

It is important to understand that leaders must instill and maintain discipline and that discipline is in fact a function of command. However, inexperienced supervisors sometimes equate discipline with punishment. Discipline has nothing to do with punishment and everything to do with structure, order, planning, and quality of service as well as organizational and personal integrity. These things are necessary for any organization to be successful. *Discipline* as defined by the dictionary is a noun, meaning "training to act in accordance with the rules; an activity or exercise or regimen that develops or improves a skill or training."[4] Organizational discipline is not a list of "Thou Shall Not's"; it is, however an understanding and an *expectation* of what the employee(s) role is, what he or she is expected to conform to, and that his or her actions must be in line with the mission and values of the organization. Employees and team members, in any organization, have to understand that they are accountable to the leader/supervisor and the organization. The leader is ultimately responsible for the direction of the team or the group. The leader must ensure that the team or group is in line with the organization's mission and strategic plan. He or she is constantly making corrections, much like a pilot or a boat captain, in order to stay on course. It is, therefore, the responsibility of leaders to articulate their expectations to the employee, team, or group. Those expectations should align with the core values and mission of the organization. This is a dynamic element of organizational discipline.

For a new leader or supervisor, this can be challenging because many new supervisors believe that their subordinates share their passion and drive for the organization. I recall a warning given to me by my former group supervisor, Ron D'Ulisse, prior to me reporting to my first supervisory position in Newark, New Jersey. "Capra, your biggest problem is that you believe everyone feels the same way about work as you do!" He was right; I did believe that, but now my interaction with Billy was challenging that belief. Yet I was still convinced (at least initially) that I could help Billy get his discipline back, that I somehow would be able to "fix" Billy.

CHAPTER 3

THE BAGGAGE FACTOR

S A NEWLY MINTED LEADER, I initially believed it was part of my job to fix people—that is, for those subpar performers, I would somehow, through sheer will and charisma on my part, turn them into outstanding employees. You know what I am talking about; you've seen the ads for some leadership courses: "Turn your poor employees into outstanding performers!" Sounds great, but I soon learned leaders are not called to "fix" anyone, despite what the motivational posters or courses seem to describe. You see, leaders must deal with what I call "the Baggage Factor." That is, all of our people come with baggage (I include myself in this), both good and bad. Their personalities, characters, and work ethics are usually in place when they come to our organization. Their perception of the world is often shaped by their beliefs and, to some extent, their generational experience. Your job as a leader is not to fix them, largely because you can't put something in someone that wasn't there in the first place! However, as a leader, your people must know about your expectations—what you expect of them, what the organization expects of them, and what they can expect from you.

My brother Mike is the superintendent of the infamous Sing-Sing State Prison located in Ossining, New York. Mike is an incredibly gifted and passionate leader, who started his career over thirty years ago as a nineteen-year-old correction officer. Mike has made it a habit to meet with every newly promoted sergeant, lieutenant, and captain who works under his command. He does so not only to congratulate him or her, but to ensure that as leaders, those individuals understand what he expects from them and what they can expect from him. Mike routinely advises first-line leaders that their job is to *train, motivate, and supervise* members of their respective teams—a very simple yet pointed expectation that he discusses in detail with his leaders.

I have learned throughout my years in leadership positions that organizational members need to fully understand and appreciate what is expected of them—and not just when they arrive in an organization; they should be routinely reminded of these expectations. It is critical to ensure that your subordinates understand your expectations and that your expectations coincide with the organization's mission, vision, and values. Your expectations to members of your team, section, squad, group, and organization as a whole must be clear and concise. You must be sure that those you have charge over understand where you stand on almost everything. As a first-line supervisor, you are the face of your organization. If you do not agree with and promote the mission and values of your organization, you are already doomed to fail as both a manager and as an emerging leader.

During my tenure as a DEA group supervisor, I was explaining the then-difficult process of how to calculate the amount of per diem on a voucher that a relatively new young agent was entitled to during his temporary duty assignment. I explained that if the agent left before 6:00 a.m., he was entitled to a full day's per diem. (This accounted for approximately $26.00) However, if he left after 6:00 a.m., the agent was entitled to $19.50. This new agent was a fairly cocky but experienced law enforcement officer. Following my explanation, the young agent looked left and then right at which time he smiled, winked, and smugly stated, "Yeah, I left before six ..." I immediately became infuriated with his response for a number of reasons. First, he assumed I wouldn't care that he was trying to get over for $6.50; second, he assumed, based on his demeanor and comment, that I would approve. I immediately leaned into him, and using a string of profanities that would make a sailor blush (again, I hadn't read any good leadership books yet), I explained that anything he put in my inbox, I would assume was truthful and accurate. But the moment I thought his integrity was in question, I would do everything I could to ensure he was fired. I went on to explain that anyone who was willing to get fired over $6.50 was capable of any number of atrocities. Further, I exclaimed to him that I did not lie, cheat, or steal and absolutely would not tolerate anyone else who did under my command. He sat up straight and assured me that he absolutely understood. His voucher submission subsequently reflected that he departed after noon. Now, I was left with two options: look over this agent's shoulder on every move, or begin to trust that he was trying to be cute and now realized the significance of my position as well as our agency's position on integrity and character. I decided on the latter. (As a follow-up, this agent is now one of the most talented and gifted professionals in the outfit.)

The importance of articulating expectations is really quite simple; we are attempting to develop habits of excellence with our people, and in doing so, we reinforce those same habits within ourselves as leaders. I am routinely asked how to begin to accomplish this. I proffer the following questions: Do you know your organization? What is your mission? What is your organization's vision? What does your organization value? Now, can you distill these important principles for your people to understand and appreciate? For example DEA has, like many organizations, a five-year strategic plan that outlines all of the above questions. Within the framework of this strategic plan are the processes we are to execute in order to reach our goals. Unfortunately, it is a very detailed and verbose document and it would be foolish of us as leaders to expect our people to memorize this plan. However, I am able to simplify our mission in terms they will remember and pass on to others. For instance, in meeting with our people, I routinely remind them: "We are the Drug Enforcement Administration; our job is to take dope off the street and put bad people in jail. We are men and women who represent the finest attributes of public service; we are men and women of integrity, character, and honor who daily strive to serve and protect members of our communities against criminal organizations. Our quest is for excellence in all that we do, both professionally and personally!"

Over and over again, I remind our people of this, both new employees and those who are very senior. At every opportunity, I encourage them not to be content but to continue to reach up and strive for excellence. I want this to sink down into their respective beings and become a part of who they are, of who we are, to instill pride, meaning, and purpose and to continually develop habits of excellence. Bob Vernon, a retired assistant police chief for the Los Angeles Police Department, says of excellence: "Excellence is superior to success. To some people, success means winning at all costs. It can spawn an unhealthy competitive spirit that's ultimately destructive." Vernon goes on to describe how a person can actually succeed without ever pursuing excellence. Pursuing excellence requires one to continually seek to improve—all the time![5]

There is a tactical axiom that states if you "train the way you fight, you will fight the way you train." It is really akin to reaping what you sow by pouring meaning and life into the men and women you have responsibility for so that they understand and begin to appreciate the importance of their respective positions in the organization. So our mission is not to "fix" someone but to ensure that those we have a responsibility for understand our expectations, and this is done as frequently as possible in an attempt to help them grow as professionals. My good friend Coach Rod Olson describes this as pouring greatness into the lives of the people around us in order to take them to a place they can't get to by themselves.[6] In his book *Servant Leadership in the Boardroom*, Dr. Kent Keith states that "… organizations cannot meet the needs of customers without meeting the needs of their employees, colleagues, or associates who actually provide the programs, products or service … they also need meaning and purpose in their lives."[7] So I submit that part of a leader's responsibility is to grow his or her people. In doing so, a leader helps the organization flourish.

But, you ask, what if you are busy pouring into someone only to see that it is quickly leaking out the back end? Good question. I have a somewhat simple solution. I often advise leaders not to waste time with your 10 percent. In other words, if I see that time and time again, what I am pouring into someone is leaking out of his or her back end, I no longer waste precious time on the individual. Such people routinely account for about 10 percent of the people we work with. This does not mean that I suddenly treat the individual as a piece of garbage or that I necessarily ignore his or her existence. It means that I understand that the person may not be interested in growing professionally—or personally, for that matter. He or she shows no interest in developing better skills. Maybe the person is simply task oriented. "Give me a task, and I complete it, over and done, nothing further." It doesn't mean that because an individual is task oriented he or she is not valuable to the organization. It means that you as the leader recognize that pouring time and energy into him or her for the purposes of growth is a waste of time.

There is an axiom in management and leadership courses that states "the best predictor of an individual's future performance is past performance!" In other words, a leopard doesn't change its spots! Cruel you say? What about all those books and courses on making a poor performer into an outstanding employee? Here is what I have learned: anyone who attempts to tell you that you can "fix" an employee's work ethic, character, or attitude with three simple steps is about to sell you some magic beans! I remind you of the "baggage factor" and that people come to us with certain baggage. *You can't put something in someone that wasn't there in the first place.* This doesn't mean that these people won't function as workers, just that you shouldn't waste your valuable time on those who leak! Every organization has such individuals. In DEA, I call them "shoe salesmen." They shouldn't be here, and this is not their calling. Oh, they function, but they would do a better job as a shoe salesman than as law enforcement professionals.

During one afternoon, Matt, one of my agents, walked into my office to discuss the possibility of leaving a little early on Friday so he could see his kid's soccer game. (As a side note, DEA agents are required to work on average a ten-hour day; however, the normal workday can be anywhere from a twelve- to eighteen-hour day, depending on the investigation or the enforcement operations.) For me, Matt's request was a no-brainer. I told him not to worry about it and to make sure he made his kid's game in plenty of time. As the month went by, I began to notice that Matt was now leaving early almost every Friday. I decided to call Matt into my office on a Monday morning to ask about this, and without any hesitation, he told me that he was coaching his kid's soccer team so he needed to leave early on Fridays. I must have had a weird look on my face because Matt then said, "Besides, you are the one who told us not to disregard our families!"

I jumped up and threw what I call the "BS flag" and then started to tell him the difference between disregarding his family and ignoring his employment responsibilities. I then, in a not-so-nice sort of tone (just started reading *Lincoln on Leadership*) began to go over my expectations for him as an agent in the group and what organizational discipline required. I also told him quite pointedly that balance with his family responsibilities did not mean that his work life had to suffer; balance meant just that—*balance*. I would soon realize that when I attempted to pour good stuff into Matt, he simply "leaked" it out of his backside … "baggage factor."

Sometimes, leaders can make the mistake of misjudging a subordinate because of his or her willingness to question a leader's decision or a course of action. Just before arriving at the Dallas Field Division, I was contacted by Billy "Bubba" Bryant. Billy and I had served in headquarters together, and he was now the assistant special agent in charge of Little Rock, Arkansas. Billy was and still is an outstanding leader who is greatly loved and respected by all who know him. As I answered the phone, I heard Billy in his Southern twang say, "Hey, big head [a loving term of endearment he had for me], you are going to meet Ricky Smith in Dallas. Listen, he's a crime fighter; he's been around a long time, and you can count on him!" This was Billy's way of telling me that Ricky was an outstanding agent, end of story.

I soon learned that Ricky was a very senior agent who had more time on the job than most of the leaders in the division. He was a talented professional and was highly respected in the law enforcement community for his investigative abilities as well as his tactical and technical expertise. There was also something else about Ricky that was undeniable; Ricky loved his profession, and he loved the people he worked with every day. Anytime someone had a personal illness, tragedy, or any problem, Ricky was usually the first person on the scene to comfort and support those who were in need. Ricky could have easily risen up through the ranks in leadership, but he loved being on the street and decided many years ago not to pursue the management path. Yet there were some leaders who described Ricky as distant and somewhat antimanagement. This was because Ricky never hesitated to speak up if he thought there might be a better way to do things or if he thought someone had been wronged or mistreated. Instead of leveraging this seasoned agent's wisdom and knowledge, some counted it as insubordination and antimanagement behavior. The more I got to know Ricky, the more I realized how valuable he was, not only as an agent, but as a highly regarded mentor and informal leader in the division. He soon became my "go-to" guy; every time a supervisor rotated out of the division, it was Ricky who would be asked to lead the group until a new supervisor arrived, always with the same request, "Ricky, I need you to keep this crew safe and active."

Ricky would always respond, "Boss, I would be honored to ..." He was and still is an amazing professional and a good friend.

The point here is that as leaders, we need to be open and willing to listen and not to fear or for that matter be intimidated by those who question our decisions. An important part of establishing a relationship with the men and women in your organization is being able to leverage their talent in pursuing your mission. Therefore, leaders need to be secure in their own maturity and identity as well as recognize the expertise and maturity of those they lead. As an example, I was talking to a young supervisor who was describing a major disagreement he had had with one of his agents. During the conversation, the supervisor, without any hesitation, stated, "Boss, he earned the right to disagree with me based on his expertise and seniority." The supervisor afforded the senior agent the opportunity, given the particular circumstances, to voice his opinion and in doing so, validated the value and significance the agent held with his leader. (I can hear my father's voice telling me, "There is always someone faster, stronger, smarter, and better-looking than you, so you better be willing and able to accept that when you see it ...").

CHAPTER 4

DOING THE RIGHT THING

HOW MANY OF YOU HAVE heard the phrase "managers do things right; leaders do the right thing"? What does that mean? Really, I'm asking, what the heck does this mean? I often pose these questions to my audience: Does this mean leaders don't do things right? Do managers not do the right thing? The poster, in my opinion, is another nice piece of wall art you can hang in your office that will gather dust like your singing fish.

The number-one reason people leave an organization is not salary; it is the lack of value one feels in a given organization. Salary or money is usually way down the list of reasons people leave. Typically, this lack of value is described in terms like: "My boss doesn't care about me. I have no sense of belonging or growth. This place is so sterile. It's all about the profit. It's all about the mission." My friend Coach Rod Olson says that "a great leader has the ability to capture the hearts of his or her people!"[8] You can capture their hearts by having a heart for them. In other words, leaders need to learn how to fall in love with their people. Often, when I talk about loving your people, audiences (especially warriors) start to at first look a little uncomfortable. I am not talking about kumbaya or dandelions in your hair. I am talking about the importance of truly understanding that people in any organization should come first and everything else is second; you see, love is a conscious act of your will, and I submit it is necessary to understanding what "doing the right thing" really means.

One of the best lessons we have in our culture on love and doing the right thing lies in the biblical story of the Good Samaritan:

> A certain man was going down from Jerusalem to Jericho, and he fell among robbers, who both stripped him and beat him, and departed, leaving him half dead. By chance a certain priest was going down that way. When he saw him, he passed by on the other side. In the same way a Levite also, when he came to the place, and saw him, passed by on the other side. But a certain Samaritan, as he travelled, came where he was. When he saw him, he was moved with compassion, came to him, and bound up his wounds, pouring on oil and wine. He set him on his own animal, and brought him to an inn, and took care of him. On the next day, when he departed, he took out two denarii, and gave them to the host, and said to him, "Take care of him. Whatever you spend beyond that, I will repay you when I return."9

Yes, the story is about the kindness of a stranger, but there is so much more that is often missed in the story. You see, according to historians and scholars, during the first century, the Jewish people and the Samaritans from Samaria held a deep-rooted hatred for each other so great that they would avoid each other's country. Bible scholars often point out that the man who was robbed was likely a Jewish man who was traveling from Jerusalem. The priest and the Levite, members of a religious sect, again, likely from the same region, saw the injured man and passed him on the other side of the road, meaning they went out of their way to avoid the injured man. It was the Samaritan who had compassion and helped the injured man, and he did so unconditionally, meaning the Samaritan did not expect anything in return for his actions. "On the next day, when he departed, he took out two denarii, and gave them to the host, and said to him, 'Take care of him. Whatever you spend beyond that, I will repay you when I return.'"

Again, leadership is a heart thing; it starts with an understanding that people in our organization have value; they have meaning and purpose. If you wrap your arms around this principle, you will begin to understand the "how-to" of loving them. I will also add that the essence of leading unconditionally means that you don't expect anything in return. In other words, it's not about *you* as the beneficiary; unconditional leadership requires one to have a heart for his/her people, to strive to make a difference in the lives of those one serves. If you truly want to make a positive difference in your organization, learn to fall in love with those you have been entrusted to lead. Now, please understand, love can be very uncomfortable because it requires honesty, tact, consistency, and a constant drive for excellence.

The famous Dallas Cowboys football coach Tom Landry said that his job was to "get players to do sometimes what they don't want to do so that they can become what they want to become."[10] In other words, his job was to constantly push them in practice, to establish workout routines that developed strength and endurance, to get them to memorize and practice intricate plays that became instinctual on the grid-iron, and to instill discipline on and off the field with the goal of becoming a championship football team. I submit to you that Coach Landry loved his players and his team.

So the question is—or should be—"Where do I start with this whole unconditional leading and loving thing?" You start by developing trust. In order to develop trust, you need to develop a relationship with those you serve. Ken Blanchard states that "when you learn to lead another person, you learn about building trust. Without trust, it is impossible for an organization to function effectively."[11]

So trust requires a relationship, and a relationship requires you to get to know your people—I mean *really* know them, their professional desires, their personal lives, their family circumstances, and their beliefs. Now, guaranteed, this is not a requirement for any leader. You won't find this on any organization mission or values statement; in fact, you will not find this as a requirement in any business course. But if you want to make a difference in your organization, if you want to make a difference in the lives of those you are entrusted to lead, and if you want to make a difference in your own leadership walk, get to really know your people!

Getting to know people well is no easy task and is not accomplished overnight. I am not saying that you have to send birthday cards to your people. I am not nor have I ever been the birthday boss. (I can't remember my six kids' birthdays half the time.) That being said, I have developed a habit of asking those I meet in my organization to tell me about themselves, no kidding. I ask about their families, their schooling, their parents, where they live, where they grew up. I find even with an incredibly diverse workforce that sharing personal experiences with each other can often foster a sense of community and begin to develop trust over a short period of time.

Vince was a young agent recently assigned to my enforcement group during my tenure in New Jersey. He was a passionate and focused agent who also had a lot of law enforcement experience as a former uniformed Secret Service agent. After about six months in the group, I began to notice that Vince always seemed to be going at Mach speed. What I mean is he starting getting to work before everyone else and would often be the last agent to leave late at night. I knew Vince to be a family man and that his wife recently gave birth to his son. During one late afternoon, I called him into my office to talk about his family. As the conversation went on, I suddenly stopped him midspeech and told him he needed to take some time off and go home. He immediately replied how it was his desire to be the best possible agent in DEA. I told him that I appreciated his passion and drive, but I was concerned that he might become unbalanced. He assured me this wasn't the case, at which point, I told him the following, "Vince, if you and your wife start having marital problems because of work, I am going to rip your head off!" (Now again, I didn't read that in any leadership book, but I wanted him to know that I was serious.) Almost every night for the next few months, I would yell to Vince to "Go home!" and he would routinely say, "I'm right behind you, boss." But Vince wasn't right behind me; I knew that, and it worried me.

Sometime later in the year, Vince walked into my office with a very serious and concerned look on his face. I knew intuitively what was happening with him. "Boss, I have to take some time off ... My wife and I are having some problems." His statement was met with me letting loose a tirade of profanities (still working on chapter 3 of *Lincoln*). I was yelling at him saying, "I told you not to let this happen!" I did though immediately calm down. I looked at him and simply told him to take as much time as he wanted. The good news is that Vince did become a very well-balanced professional. He is currently an outstanding supervisor, and his family life continues to thrive and be well.

After speaking to a recently promoted class of group supervisors, I was contacted by a young supervisor who asked the following: "Can I be friends with the men and women in my group?" My response was, "Absolutely, but you are their leader first." I have been told by many colleagues that they were not interested in being "friends" with their subordinates because "familiarity breeds contempt" and we as leaders become vulnerable. Therefore, they believe, it is best to keep those you lead at a distance. And I say, vulnerable to what? Vulnerable to someone taking advantage of your position on caring? Vulnerable to someone in your organization letting you down? Vulnerable to the fact that caring may, just may, initially influence you about a person's true character? If you keep people at a distance, you will never develop a relationship. If you never develop a relationship, you will never develop trust, and if you never develop trust, how then will you make a difference in the lives of those we serve and in the life of an organization? Good leaders always, always, always pay a price to lead, especially when they learn to lead unconditionally.

Dr. Kent Keith is a renowned author and international public speaker on servant leadership. In 1968, at the age of nineteen, Dr. Keith published *Anyway: The Paradoxical Commandments*,[12] which became a national bestseller and was translated into sixteen languages. These paradoxical commandments speak to the heart and meaning of unconditional love and service, such as *"People are illogical, unreasonable, and self-centered. Love them anyway."* As leaders, we would do well to have the next generation of leaders memorize and recite these commandments daily.

I submit that leaders should hold a passionate desire for their people to succeed both at work and in their personal lives. If the people we serve are broken at home, ultimately, they will be broken at work, so their all-around well-being should be important to all of us as leaders, no matter where we are on the leadership ladder. Getting to know our people also gives us insight into their lives and becomes important when we start to observe or notice a change in their work life. Why is this important? Because in pursuing a career, in pursuing a calling, life happens! In what chapter of any leadership book will you find the easy steps on how to handle the loss of a spouse or a child, the diagnosis of an illness, a divorce, or any number of tragedies or events that beset our people on a daily basis? There are none, but a relationship with your people helps you to deal with these issues head-on. I didn't say it would be easy or always successful, but a real relationship gives you, as the leader, the courage to step in and be part of the support mechanism when life suddenly kicks in the door. That, my friends, is love, and that is what doing the right thing is sometimes all about.

CHAPTER 5

MORAL LEADERSHIP

WHILE THIS NOTION OF HAVING a heart for people may be foreign to some leaders, I will submit that it can't be faked; oh sure, some leaders may go a little while hiding their character or real motives for assuming a leadership position, but there is an old saying that goes "You can fool some of the people some of the time, but you can't fool all of the people all of the time!" That's because we as humans have an uncanny ability to see through insincerity or stage presence (acting). Ultimately, the true character of a leader or organization as a whole comes to the surface. Let me try to elaborate somewhat. Every organization has a belief system in place, and most have it written down in terms of a mission statement followed by a values statement. Many values statements identify the organization's beliefs in terms of how they view their respective customers, products, and employees. But my question to leaders is this: are those values borne out in the actions of the organizational leadership team? Words have meaning, and leaders must know what they believe!

One of my favorite youth counselors and authors is Josh McDowell. Josh often challenges young men and women to know what they believe and understand that their actions always identify their beliefs.[13] This is because at the very core of our being, our beliefs—our deeply entrenched, hardwired beliefs—always birth what we truly value. Our beliefs and values are hidden or invisible to others. As I have stated earlier, organizational beliefs are routinely found in a values statement. However, these same beliefs and values are ultimately fleshed out consistently by a leader's actions, and it is our actions that ultimately define our character. This is not only true for a leader but for all people. Even in our daily life, we often see others who routinely say one thing but do another. Their actions speak to their character.

In pulling all of this together, we can see how a leader's actions really represent the character of an organization as seen through the eyes of employees. So if a leader's actions are inconsistent with his or her expectations, if they are inconsistent with the stated mission and values of the organization, it will begin to unravel the foundation of trust among the workforce, which will ultimately impact organizational morale and productivity. For instance, if, as a leader, you remind your people how much you value their feedback, yet you have a habit of chopping people's heads off when they provide feedback, how will you ever develop trust? If you can't develop trust, what is likely to be the climate of your organization, section, or group? Behavior such as this will start to erode a leader's moral and ethical positioning.

That being said, what does it mean to be an ethical or moral leader? When I bring this subject up, I am always amazed to see how uncomfortable some organizational executives become in discussing the principles of ethics and morality. This is largely due to the fact that they do not understand what the terms mean. Words have meanings, and they are sometimes lost in our vernacular because of misperceptions.

The word *morality* is a noun, defined as "conformity to the rules of right conduct."[14] The word *moral* is an adjective, defined as "… concerned with the principles or rules of right conduct or the distinction between right and wrong; ethical." Yet we often hear people exhort that we can't push "our" morality on someone else or question who exactly determines the type of morality to follow, or better yet, state that each person must determine his or her own morality, but is that correct? Of course not, this is a recipe for disaster in any organization and above all in a free society. Our entire American legal system and the codification of our statutes are based on ethical principles and the moral law. Ah, but what is the "moral law"? According to Dr. Norman Geisler, the moral law is "the law not everyone obeys, but the law by which everyone expects to be treated."[15]

Our democratic society has determined that individuals are expected to act and behave a certain way for the safety, health, and welfare of our citizenry and country. While our nation is based upon the principle that all men and women are endowed with inalienable rights, this does not mean that individuals can have it their way or can do whatever they want in a free society. To suggest that they can and will is nothing more than the imposition of radical autonomy. The emphasis on radical autonomy in our society is symptomatic of an entitlement generation. That is to say, we have in this current generation, many (not all) men and women who are, by all accounts, spoiled and believe that the world owes them something or that they are entitled and demand things they want, not what they necessarily need. (This may be more symptomatic of the breakdown of the American family, but that is a topic for another book.)

Radical autonomy left unchecked will lead to chaos, which leads to anarchy. When anarchy reigns in a society, it will give rise to a dictator. A dictatorship government will give rise to despotism, which ultimately outlaws freedom and enslaves people. We need only apply the radical autonomy theory to any organization to see the devastating consequences. Just think if all employees decided individually, for themselves, what was right or wrong with the organization: loss of focus, loss of vision, loss of direction, loss of control, and ultimately the death of the organization. The same can be said for a society. So leaders need to be morally sound and willing to be the example in order to establish the moral climate in any organization. And leaders need not only to hire moral men and women but to routinely articulate and enforce the moral underpinnings in their respective organizations.

Narcotics agents and officers operate in extremely hostile environments, and the bad guys we target are some of the worst criminals on the face of the planet. Most major traffickers have no regard for life, liberty, or the rule of law. Their sole purpose is to make money off the backs of addicted victims in order to live an opulent and obscene lifestyle. They will torture, maim, or murder anyone, including a family member, who gets in the way of their ability to make a buck. There is always a bullet or a jail cell waiting for them, usually right around the corner. As a result of working in this arena, it has been often incorrectly stated or portrayed that narcotics units tend to have a corruption issue because of the amount of money (millions of dollars) that they come across during their respective investigations. Narcotics officers are routinely portrayed as immoral or unethical individuals slightly above the bad guys we go after. This is far, far from the actual truth. I have been blessed to work with some of the finest men and women serving as leaders in narcotics units around the world—men and women who define service, honor, integrity, and daily demonstrate outstanding moral and ethical behavior.

In late September 1989, my group and a team of narcotics agents from five different police departments executed a search warrant on a warehouse in Sylmar, California. Inside the warehouse, we located over twenty-one tons of cocaine and just over twelve million dollars in cash. The cocaine was secreted in numerous cardboard boxes located on thirty-six separate pallets, and the cash was located in numerous gym bags and boxes. Some of the bags were open, exposing tens of thousands of dollars for all to see. Realizing the enormity of the seizure, Sgt. Andy Key immediately took charge of the location by securing the facility, placing an armed perimeter around the scene, and establishing a sign-in sheet for all who came in and out of the warehouse. Several dozen agents and detectives worked on processing the scene and following up on the investigation through the night. At around 3:00 a.m., I sat down in the midst of the excitement and the investigation to wrap my head around what we had done, and then I saw it; Sgt. Key was collecting a couple of bucks from some of the other law enforcement leaders on the scene so he could have one of his patrolmen buy some coffee for the officers and agents working in the warehouse. I remember smiling and thinking to myself, *We are surrounded by millions of dollars of drug money, and instead, Andy is reaching into his pocket in order to take care of this crew.* It would have been easy to grab a couple of exposed twenty-dollar bills, and most people outside our profession would never have thought twice about that. Many would have said that he would be morally justified, but that was not Sgt. Andy Key; he represented his police department. He represented and exemplified character and integrity; he represented what right moral conduct meant, not just as a police officer, but as a leader in his organization. You see, Andy understood that "others came first" but not at the expense of expediency, not at the expense of his character, and not at the expense of tarnishing his shield or his integrity as a public servant and a law enforcement leader.

Unfortunately, there have been numerous examples of leaders who go down as failures as a result of their moral misconduct. We have witnessed not only businessmen but politicians, community leaders, clergy, and public servants who fail miserably because of the compromise of their moral fabric. Some experts describe these compromises and failures as moral viruses. These leaders willingly allow the virus to take hold of them for selfish motives, such as greed, pleasure, or fear. I submit that the reason that moral viruses take hold is the inability to keep one's ego in check. This will give rise to an ethically challenged leader.

We need to have a healthy ego, as the ego is necessary for confidence and self-esteem. However, leaders who lose control of their egos and begin to develop an arrogant attitude see themselves as more important than the people around them or, for that matter, more important than the organization as a whole. When the leader starts to take hold of this selfish arrogance, it is not unusual to see him or her begin to use the organization as a means to accomplish selfish desires. Suddenly, the rules don't apply to him or her. In *How the Mighty Fail*, author Jim Collins states, "To use the organization primarily as a vehicle to increase your own personal success—more wealth, more fame, and more power—at the expense of its long-term success is undisciplined,"[16] and I would add immoral and unethical. Good and effective leaders must have a big dose of humility when serving others.

In their book *Start with Humility*, Merwyn Hayes and Michael Comer interviewed numerous CEOs on building trust and inspiring followers. Throughout the book, the authors related example after example of how some of the most impactful organizational leaders consistently displayed humility in the workplace. They also cited numerous warnings by these leaders regarding an ego left unchecked. A Roche Pharmaceutical executive Bill Burns was quoted:

> You have to keep your feet on the ground when others want to put you on a pedestal. After a while on a pedestal, you stop hearing the truth. It's filtered by the henchmen, and they read you so well they know what you want to hear. You end up as the queen bee in the hive, with no relationship with the worker bees.[17]

Leadership positions come with authority and power, which may attract people for all the wrong reasons. (Again, what is your motive to lead?) Many times, leaders reach "celebrity" status, which can be challenging for anyone in that position. I often start out my presentations with a comical statement that goes, "I am sort of a big deal at work!" In the midst of the audience's laughter, I reiterate over and over again, "Really, really, I am very important!" This is routinely followed by changing expressions, inquisitively looking to see if I am serious. When the audience quiets, I typically state, "Beware of the ego! He will take you to a place filled with false promises and ideas; beware of the quiet lies he tells to you, how important you are, how the organization can't survive without you!" If the ego is not held in check, it will corrupt a leader's values and can lead to unethical behavior.

So how do we as leaders ensure we don't fall into the trap of an out-of-control ego? We must continually be willing to develop habits of excellence. It has been said that when people shape their habits, their habits then begin to shape them. There is an old Jewish proverb that states: "Do nothing out of selfish ambition or vain conceit. Rather, in humility, value others above yourselves, not looking to your own interests but each of you to the interests of the others."[18]

Unethical behavior demonstrated by a leader will erode trust; unethical behavior tolerated by a leader will lead to a corrupt unit, group, section, or entire organization. Corruption brings to mind such things as theft, bribery, and the like and certainly can be and has been the result of unethical behavior. But what I am really talking about is corruption in terms of loss of organizational discipline, loss of personal discipline; instead of selfless behavior, selfish behavior begins to rule, which erodes personal dignity and breaks down the integrity of a team, section, or the organization as a whole. Over the course of time, if such unethical behavior is not addressed, it will lead to personal and organizational failure. We refer to this often as the "slippery slope." So what then constitutes unethical behavior? Really, again, I am asking you, what do you define as unethical behavior, and what are you as a leader willing to tolerate?

Certainly, we would all agree that stealing, lying, and cheating at work is wrong and in fact can be construed as criminal conduct—and therefore is unethical—but what about immoral conduct? Right now, there are some of you who are thinking, *See, it's this morality thing! You are trying to force your morality on others!* Before you get too overheated, let's remember that *words have meaning*. The term *immoral* is an adjective, defined as "violating moral principles."[19] Another definition is "not conforming to the patterns of conduct usually accepted or established as consistent with principles of personal and social ethics." In failing to address this "nonconformity," leaders try to hide behind the myth that they are not in a position to define moral or immoral behavior because, well, quite frankly, everyone is doing it … What a crock! In the words of my former college professor and retired New York City Police Detective Vince Cookingham, "Just because everyone is doing it doesn't mean it's right."[20]

While sitting at my desk one morning, I began to hear a young agent bragging quite loudly about his after-work liaisons with a well-endowed dancer (you are starting to get uncomfortable). As he spoke, my stomach began to turn because the agent had a wonderful wife and family who routinely attended group barbecues at my house. As his conversation went on with subsequent laughter coming from other agents in the group, I struggled internally with the issue. I tried to convince myself that if he wanted to ruin his family life, well, that was his decision and it should be of little concern for me. *Besides*, I thought, *who am I to tell him what to do after work?* But the reality was that my refusal to act had nothing to do with a moral dilemma; it had to do with the fact that at the time, I lacked the *moral courage* to act! You see, quite honestly, I was too afraid of what he and others might think to act unconditionally. At that unique time, I had the ability to impact the life of the agent involved, but I also missed the opportunity to reinforce what I often spoke about: family values and balance. I let fear steer my actions or lack thereof. Moral courage is a willingness to step out of one's safe zone and does not suggest there is an absence of fear; it is deciding and understanding at the moment that something is more important than fear itself. While I can never get that moment back, I promised myself that I would never let another opportunity like that go by unaddressed.

We need to be willing to be courageous with our thoughts, our feelings, and our emotions, and it often is a personal struggle. However, as leaders, we must not be afraid to demonstrate moral courage, which allows us not only to walk away from situations that tempt our ego but to address unethical and immoral behavior by members of our organization. Why? Because we should desire for our people to succeed in their given profession and in their personal lives. When they do so, our organizations will flourish. Study after study demonstrates that organizations and families who stress and demonstrate good moral behavior are more likely to succeed than those that do not. Moral courage is being committed to what we know is right and true, even when it is difficult, even if it means we may be ridiculed and outcast. Finally, demonstrating moral courage may require a leader—or for that matter anyone in the organization—to put it all on the line for choosing right behavior and good moral positioning.

CHAPTER 6

THROWING A LIFE RING INSTEAD OF AN ANVIL

P**ICTURE THE FOLLOWING:** A**T A** leadership conference, a number of first-line supervisors are discussing issues concerning their respective agents. During the conversation, one of the supervisors brings up the fact that Johnny, one of his outstanding agents, was metaphorically driving toward the cliff at ninety miles per hour! All the supervisors began to pipe up with comments like, "Yeah, Johnny, he's great, but you're right; he's heading toward that cliff all right. What a shame! He's really a good agent. Yep, good guy, but what can we do? He's a big boy, but he is close to going over the edge … Yeah, too bad!" Now I ask you: Is that you? Have you ever been a part of this type of discussion? I would be willing to bet that either as a leader or a member of any team, we have all witnessed the guy or gal who was heading toward the cliff. The problem is that too many leaders or, for that matter, members of a team, group, or section will sit back and watch Johnny drive off the cliff, and then only when he crashes on the bottom, react. And how do we react when Johnny crashes? We throw the anvil of discipline or termination on top of him while he is burning up … Ahh, now that's effective leadership!

When I arrived at my first field command as the special agent in charge of the Dallas Field Division, I immediately met with all my senior leaders and told them what I expected of them and what they could expect from me. Senior leaders within DEA Field Division are usually identified as assistant special agents in charge (ASACs). These leaders routinely have responsibility for several enforcement groups, sections, and entire offices within the divisional area of responsibility (AOR). The Dallas AOR encompassed the Northern and Eastern Districts of Texas as well as the state of Oklahoma. Although having one of the larger geographical areas, the Dallas Field Division was one of the smallest field divisions in terms of numbers of agents and personnel assigned in the domestic arena. I was fortunate in that I had already either worked with or knew my senior leaders for several years and they were, in their own rights, outstanding professionals who had a passion to serve and to lead. My vision for the field division was to "pursue excellence both professionally and personally; that we (Dallas Field Division) would be an example for other divisions to follow and that we would be viewed by the public we serve as the example of good government!" I have always believed that excellence and the pursuit of excellence were critical elements in growing a successful organization.

As a part of their responsibility, I challenged my senior leaders to really get to know their people and to subsequently challenge their first-line leaders to do the same. On an almost daily basis, the senior leadership would remind their respective leadership staff about caring for their people; they reminded them of the importance of establishing a relationship of trust, loving them, and caring for their respective well-being all while pursuing excellence. This expectation was a priority as was the expectation of an outstanding level of technical, investigative, and tactical competence in the execution of our law enforcement responsibilities. So there became an intricate weaving of all of these expectations and responsibilities; you could not pursue one without the others.

After about six months, I asked one of my senior ASACs, Dan Salter, now the special agent in charge of Dallas, if our men and women of the division were getting it. Did they understand the importance of what we were trying to establish within this command? Were they starting to absorb what I described in the pursuit of our vision? Dan looked at me, smiled, and then said, "No, not yet." I calmly responded, "Okay," but in my head I was screaming, *Not yet! What does he mean not yet? How could they not get it yet? Come on, really?* While I recognized that turning the battleship takes a little time, inside, I wanted my vision to catch fire overnight, which is an unreasonable expectation because organizational habits are developed over time.

Fast-forward to one morning two years after my arrival, Dan walked into my office and stated, "They are starting to get it."

Of course, I asked, "Get what?"

Dan smiled, shook his head, and then told me the following: "I had one of our young supervisors walk into my office because he needed to talk to me. The supervisor stated that he was worried about Cody, one of his agents." Dan asked what was wrong, and the supervisor simply said, "Cody is a great agent, and he has no problem in the group, but I am worried that he is burning both ends of the candle pretty hard." Dan paused and then asked the supervisor what he wanted to do, and without hesitation, the supervisor simply stated, "I am going to tell Cody that I am worried about him; that's all." Dan told the supervisor to also tell Cody that we were all worried about him. Now again, Cody was not having any issue at work; in fact, he was an outstanding agent. But the supervisor knew him and had a sense that something was off. Following the meeting with the supervisor, Cody admitted that he was having some marital problems and that he wasn't coming to grips with this issue and so was staying out late. The supervisor asked how he could help and suggested some alternatives for assistance. Cody was thankful and would tell people later how great it was to know that the leadership team really cared not just about his success at work but about his family life as well.

This was a watershed moment for our division. It was evidence that our small team was maturing into outstanding leaders who would have a positive impact on our organization now as well as in the future. Our young leaders weren't waiting for their people to crash or go over the cliff; often, they were in tune with their respective team and believed that they had a moral responsibility to step in and try to help resolve issues even though an employee might have been responsible for the decisions that led to the pending issue. But that is not always possible, and there are times when Johnny does drive off the cliff and we never see it coming. We only see the burning wreckage at the bottom and then ask, "Now what?"

Early one morning as I arrived at the division, I was called into one of my ASAC's offices. He was busy typing on his computer. The ASAC turned to me and with a very concerned look on his face relayed the following story. "Jimmy, I am sorry to report that last night, Tommy's wife threw him out of his house with all of his belongings. Tommy apparently confided to his wife that he has been dealing with some very personal demons, including issues with infidelity as well as other inappropriate activity." This was incredibly hard to hear, as I had always known Tommy to be very a concerned family man who was active with his kids and his church. My ASAC went on to say, "So I am writing up a referral memo to the Office of Professional Responsibility (OPR) for whatever action they deem appropriate."

Now, the DEA has a very strict and well understood code of conduct, and any violations of these as well as any allegations of misconduct are required to be reported to this office, which is our equivalent to internal affairs. After taking this all in, I sat back and quietly assumed that the

44

ASAC may have believed that Tommy utilized his government vehicle inappropriately and/or he utilized his government laptop to access unauthorized sites and that probably was the reason for the referral. Frustrated and severely disappointed in hearing this news, I nodded my head, turned to leave the room, and then caught myself. "Wait a minute!" I yelled. "Let me see if I got this right; we have an employee whose entire life is coming apart at the seams because he couldn't live with the guilt of the demons he was dancing with, tells his wife, who does what is natural and throws his ass out … and now we are going to light him on fire and grind him into the ground? Is that what we are doing?" The ASAC and I just looked at each other for a moment, mulling over my statement, which by now had caught the ear of the other ASACs in the office, who were now in the room. I decided that instead of reporting this to OPR, we would take a number of actions to include auditing government credit cards and computers to ensure there were no violations. Last but certainly not least, knowing Tommy's faith affiliation, I contacted our division chaplain and asked for his assistance in the matter. He promptly responded by getting Tommy some physical, mental, and spiritual assistance. We didn't crush Tommy; we didn't watch him burn up even though he was responsible for his actions. We did what we could to attempt to mitigate his self-inflicted wounds. He was and still is a member of our family who drove off the cliff. We understood as leaders that we had a duty and a moral responsibility to throw him a lifeline, and we did so quietly and unconditionally because that is what good leaders do.

So the question for some is why? I mean, why should organizational leaders care about those who make poor decisions in life and who cause themselves to implode because of their actions? I submit that we care because we need to understand that all of us as human beings have a moral purpose in life and that at times we need to consider applying the golden rule in those situations. Most people understand that the principle behind the golden rule is to do unto others as you would do unto yourself ... or something like that. However, I love how John Maxwell explains the application of the golden rule by asking the question: "How would I like to be treated in this situation?"[21] Maxwell goes on to state "... that the wonderful thing about the Golden Rule is that it makes the intangible tangible. You don't need to know the law; you don't need to explore the nuances of philosophy; you simply imagine yourself in the place of another person."[22] I point out that Maxwell does not state how I *deserve* to be treated but rather "how I would like to be treated" given the circumstances. Deserving implies that we are entitled to something. For those of us who have made mistakes, really, we are entitled to burn in the wreckage below the cliff, but we really would like someone to throw us a lifeline. The golden rule speaks to having a heart of compassion and understanding because sometimes we all need a second chance even though we may not deserve one.

It is again important that the reader fully understand that I am not suggesting by any means that when we involve ourselves as leaders in the lives of our people, that somehow, there will be a Disney ending where people go on to live happily ever after. Even if we have a heart of compassion and we do our best to apply the golden rule, it does not mean that our people will instantly be whole again. Our people may still be broken as in the case of Tommy. His life may be broken, but slowly, he is doing his best to put it back together, with the help of his work family. We recognize his life will never be the same, but we didn't walk away; we reached out to help as in any good relationship and sought to minimize the pain of his actions. As I stated in an earlier chapter, a relationship with your people helps you to deal with these issues head-on; again, it is not always easy or successful, but a real relationship gives you, as the leader, the courage to step in and be part of the support mechanism.

When the people we serve begin to realize that their leaders really care about their personal well-being, it speaks volumes into the life of an organization and becomes ingrained in the organizational culture, at first slowly. Consistent reminders by an engaged leadership team pay tremendous dividends toward motivating the workforce. Oftentimes, leaders assume that motivating the workforce is a "rah-rah" event or a kind of "up with people" theme. While these are not necessarily ineffective, they are often momentary in terms of their impact on the workforce. Then there are those who believe that a manager, supervisor, or a leader is unable to really motivate an individual employee. They posit that motivation comes from within the individual. While I do not disagree in whole with this statement, I do believe that a leader can in fact provide the opportunity for an employee to be motivated. *Motivate* is a verb, defined as "to stimulate towards action."[23] Good leaders are constantly looking for opportunities to motivate each one of their subordinates. These opportunities very often present themselves by a supervisor's actions. For example, do your subordinates know that you have their best interests at heart? Do they know that you really care about them? Do they know that you want them to succeed professionally and personally? Do they know that you get excited about their success because they make a difference? Do they know that you value them? I submit the fact that there is no better motivational tool than for people to realize that they are genuinely cared for and appreciated for their service, regardless of what their respective job may be. Doing so develops a relationship of trust.

Over the course of my three decades as a public servant, both in the uniformed military services and as a federal agent, I have witnessed a number of leaders of varying abilities ranging from the truly incompetent to the truly incredible. While there are a number of characteristics that embody great leaders, again, I submit that the number-one characteristic found in an outstanding leader is an intrinsic desire to serve the individuals he or she works with. These leaders are people of empathy and compassion who strive to make a difference. Great leaders understand that they have to make an emotional connection with organizational members. John Maxwell, a prolific leadership author and expert stated, "If you haven't taken the time to show your people that you genuinely care for their well-being, you won't be very successful in leading them, even if your motives are pure."[24] Organizations that are run by fear and intimidation are doomed to failure, and leaders who practice the same leave a legacy of chaos and anger within the organization.

Okay, I know what some of you are saying. I can hear what some of you are thinking: *So what you are telling me is as a leader, I walk in, tell my folks about my expectations, develop trust with them, tell them I care about them, fall—as you say—in love with them, and provide them with the opportunity to be motivated and then they all become perfect employees, is that it?* I wish it were that simple, but the fact is you can't just fake these things. As I stated, this never happens overnight and—here is the big thing—not everyone is going to get it; you will have "shoe salesmen." Everybody, no matter what career field, has some "shoe salesmen" in their ranks, who will never get it. I will remind you again and again that this whole leadership gig really starts with the heart of a leader, with the general understanding that people, no matter what their background, financial capacity, educational level, religious beliefs, or anything else, are the foundation of any organization and leaders have a duty and—I submit—a moral obligation to care for them, not as children, but as other human beings who have purpose in the organization and in life.

CHAPTER 7

DO YOU HAVE A WAIT PROBLEM?

I HAVE BEEN KNOWN TO ASK an audience if they have a "wait" problem. That is, do you want to make a difference in your organization, or are you waiting for someone else to make that difference? Or maybe you are the leader who tells others, "Well, when (insert *name* here) leaves, then I will be able to do (insert *what* here)," because somehow you believe that you have to "wait" until all the stars are aligned before you can exercise your gift as a leader in order to drive change in your organization. If this is the case, you will always be waiting to make a difference because you are unwilling (or lack the courage) to step out and embrace risk, which is absolutely necessary to be an effective leader. Being risk averse has a tendency to cause a leader to never challenge the status quo or for that matter, to be apprehensive in challenging a course of action because of bureaucratic policies. All organizations have some level of bureaucracy. Bureaucracy is not always bad; again, words have meaning. *Bureaucracy* defined means the strict adherence to a set of rules and/or rigid compliance with the same. Rules and rigid compliance in most cases are essential to operational effectiveness unless they fly in the face of common sense, in which case those same rigid rules become an obstruction to operational effectiveness ... confused yet?

During my assignment at Newark, New Jersey, our DEA office began the process of moving to a new location. During the move, the evidence custodian found a piece of evidence from a case that had been closed over ten years earlier. The evidence package consisted of a piece of paper that had no evidentiary value to it. The package was thought to have been destroyed several years earlier but apparently had fallen behind an evidence cabinet. After a little research, the custodian requested assistance from the duty group supervisor to prepare a very simple destruction order to dispose of the evidence properly. Instead of submitting a simple destruction document, the supervisor responded to the evidence custodian by writing a two-and-a-half-page memo citing administrative manual sections and detailing why it was neither his nor his group's responsibility to submit such documentation. When I heard about the incident, I approached the supervisor, who was an acquaintance, to ask why he thought it was necessary to respond that way. Again, he went on and on about administrative procedures and the fact that it was not his group's responsibility because it was not his investigative case or evidence, blah, blah, bublahhh! Technically, the supervisor was right, but practically and common-sense-wise, his response was cowardly and bureaucratic. I sat there for a moment thinking how perfect it would be to smack him upside his head with a plastic bat for his asinine response. It took one of my agent's five minutes to prepare a destruction order so that the custodian could properly dispose of the item in order to continue with the move of the office.

Some of you recognize this type of supervisor and are saying to yourselves, "No big deal, we all have someone like this, and besides, you said the supervisor was technically correct and the evidence was finally disposed of properly." That's not the point. You see, the evidence custodian could have simply disposed of the piece of evidence without telling anyone, but he recognized that this was an error. All he wanted to do was properly correct the error and move on, something that he needed a supervisor to assist with because it was outside of his (the custodian's) authority. Instead, his request for assistance was met with a bureaucratic roadblock, which left him with a decision either to seek additional assistance or to handle it himself (which he has no authority to do). Fortunately, the custodian decided to pursue the correct course of action. But what about next time, given a similar set of circumstances? How many times does a bureaucratic response given in order to avoid some level of risk, begin to erode organizational discipline and integrity? A little over the top, you might say. Maybe, but remember, we want to establish habits of excellence, not give our employees reasons for not complying with proper procedures because of risk-averse leaders.

In DEA, we have a saying that goes like this: "Big cases, big headaches; little cases, little headaches; no cases, no headaches!" Often, leaders in DEA recognize that the difference between big cases and little cases is the level of risk the leader and his or her team are willing to take to have the greatest impact on an investigation. Please understand that in my profession, risk is inherent in everything we do because we routinely work in a very hostile environment. Our job is to take dope off the street and put bad guys in jail, so every contact we have, whether on surveillance, search warrants, arrest warrants, or a simple interview with a suspect or witness has the potential to immediately turn into a life-and-death struggle. So we train and plan every operation with this inherent risk as a primary factor, and we do so in terms of weighing the greatest risk versus the greatest reward. Embracing risk implies that a leader must be willing to make an *active choice* that has influence on the outcome of a decision. In our profession, the decision to execute a plan of action routinely takes into account accurate information and intelligence, technical expertise and competence, availability of effective and sometimes specialized resources, and a contingency plan if and when the primary plan should start to fail.

In the spring of 1995, I received a phone call that an undercover agent had been approached by a major drug trafficker to take delivery of five thousand kilograms of cocaine and deliver the load to the Los Angeles area. Once in the Los Angeles area, the cocaine would be turned over to the traffickers, after which time, the undercover agent would receive a two-million-dollar fee for the logistical movement of the cocaine. In cases such as these, once the bad guys showed up in Los Angeles to take delivery, they would be immediately arrested, the dope would be seized, and pictures would be taken—end of case. At the time, I believed we should and could do more to expand the case. I came up with a plan that included the participation of over two hundred state, local, and federal law enforcement officers to execute the plan effectively. The reality was, however, this had never been done before. I was about to ask my superiors to let five thousand kilograms of cocaine be turned back over to the bad guys in order to expand an investigation.

When I pitched the plan to my superiors, I told them the following: "Look, why settle for arresting just two mopes who come and pick up the load? We have the opportunity to take off the entire organization. I have six fully staffed narcotics teams set up on six residences that we have located as a part of this organization. The load will likely go to one location and be broken up into these various stash pads. I have given the commanders of each of the locations full autonomy to control and execute enforcement at their given location based upon their expertise. We have a commitment from the district attorney's office and the United States Attorney's office to prepare search and arrest warrants anytime, day or night, during this operation. I have multiple helicopters for air support as well as tactical (SWAT) support from a variety of police departments that are on standby and can move on a moment's notice.

Sirs, we can do this. We have the people, we have the resources, we have the expertise … and it's worth the risk!" My superiors looked at me and smiled. They knew I was right and trusted my expertise and judgment. They were confident in my plan. (And to be really honest, they both were a little crazy anyway. No kidding, they were nuts, and I sort of played on that!)

On a beautiful Southern California morning, the undercover agent turned over five thousand kilograms of cocaine stuffed inside a forty-foot U-Haul truck to two very violent Mexican drug traffickers. From the command center located in a hotel room, I watched as the U-Haul drove away eastbound on Interstate 10 at about forty-five miles per hour followed by fifteen narcotics officers and agents, including a helicopter flying at about two thousand feet; this procession was followed by another crew of fifteen with a helicopter at 2,500 feet and a third crew and a helicopter at three thousand feet. How the bad guys didn't see us I will never know, but as I watched the procession move away, all I could think about was whether I had made the right decision. What if this failed? What if we lost the load? What if …?

Throughout the day, the operation proceeded as if the bad guys were following our script. The U-Haul truck was followed to one of the locations where it was off-loaded. The following afternoon, surveillance teams watched the cocaine loads being broken up and delivered to other previously identified locations. By late afternoon, we had identified multiple targets and additional locations, which required more teams to sit on the new locations. At the height of the operation, we estimated that we now had over three hundred law enforcement officers and agents involved with this investigation. The ballet of logistical coordination and surveillance was unlike anything we had been involved with in the past. Late in the evening, I received a call from one of the principal narcotics teams. The sergeant stated, "Jimmy, we just followed a load to a remote ranch in San Bernardino. One of my guys is low crawling in a lemon grove to get eyes on the location, but when daylight hits, we are going to be out in the open. What do you want us to do?"

Now I was quickly thinking, *What do I want to do? I want to keep going! I want to push it further! I want to ...* Then I heard myself saying, "Hey, Sarge, this is your call."

Throughout the night, we worked with the district attorney's office and the United States attorney's office to secure multiple search warrants for all the locations we had identified. At about 5:30 a.m., the radio began to crackle with excitement. From the lemon grove, the detective observed a van leaving the ranch at a high rate of speed. As the vehicle left, the driver instantly knew that he was being followed by the surveillance teams on the surrounding streets, and a brief pursuit ensued. Following the stop of the vehicle and the arrest of the suspect, detectives located multiple cell phones in the vehicle. At the time of the arrest, they correctly surmised that the suspect had warned others in the residence about his situation, but we were prepared for that. The rest of the team swarmed onto the ranch and prepared to execute the search warrant. A few minutes before 6:00 a.m., the sergeant on the scene called me to let me know "We are hitting the location." For the next three minutes, there was a deafening silence followed by an explosion of voices over the radio. "Shots fired! Shots fired! Officer down! I say again, Officer down!"

In those moments, time seems to stand still, and you find yourself wanting to race in different directions while your mind is screaming with questions: *Who is down? How many? How bad? Was this worth it?* These thoughts are immediately pushed to the side as all the training, expertise, preparation, and planning come together in a tactical and operational ballet. In the midst of ringing phones, radio chatter filled with sirens, and shouts combined with concerned voices in the command center, the order was given, "All locations, execute, execute, execute enforcement operations!" Simultaneously, in multiple locations within three counties, aircraft were launched, tactical teams initiated action, and emergency operations were immediately undertaken with exacting precision.

We would soon learn that at the ranch location, when the officers breached the door of the residence, they were met with a barrage of gunfire from a suspect who took up a tactical position about five feet from the first detective who entered the door. As the gunfire erupted from the AK-47 being fired by the suspect, the lead detective fell to the ground. Fearing that his officer had been shot, the sergeant, with no regard for his own safety, immediately placed himself between the downed officer and the suspect and began to return fire. The suspect was ultimately wounded and taken into custody. Fortunately, the officer who went down was not injured; however, he did receive powder burns from the suspect's AK-47, which initially blinded him on entry.

Within the next thirty minutes, all locations were secured and over thirty violent members of one of the largest Mexican drug-trafficking organizations were under arrest. The teams recovered all five thousand kilograms of cocaine, several million dollars in US currency, and dozens and dozens of high-caliber weapons to include several thousand rounds of ammunition, and all the good guys would be going home that night!

No one would argue that this operation was risky or that it captures the essence of a high-risk operation. However, when I speak of embracing risk, I also do so in terms of a leader evaluating and be willing to push back against procedures, guidelines, policies, and decisions that have the potential to do harm, cause confusion, and cause an organization to become mired down in processes that tend to inhibit growth and negatively impact the mission. In this case, the inherent risk of an armed and violent suspect was and is a given in our profession. Yet the bigger risk to evaluate at the time was the fact that DEA had never attempted this sort of operation before. As a matter of fact, during the height of the enforcement operation, our headquarters elements were calling in to the command center demanding to know the status of the operation because, as was briefly explained to me at the time, "you don't have our (HQ's) approval to conduct this operation!" For one thing, I told one of the callers who was a staff coordinator that I didn't need his approval. (Actually, at the time, I had no clue if I did or didn't!) I would learn that my immediate superiors, though a little crazy, knew that if certain elements in headquarters were briefed, they would never agree to letting the cocaine back into the hands of the traffickers. They evaluated the risk of conducting the operation, and they also embraced risk by pushing back against old investigative methods that produced few results.

Evaluating and embracing risk takes courage and confidence and is never done in the blind without critical evaluation and planning. As I stated earlier, embracing risk implies that a leader must be willing to make an *active choice* that has influence on the outcome of a decision. A decision to execute a plan of action should always take into account accurate information and intelligence, technical expertise and competence, availability of effective and sometimes specialized resources, and a contingency plan in addition to a number of other considerations depending on the situation at hand.

Noted author and speaker John Maxwell writes, "A ship in harbor is safe, but that's not what ships are made for."[25] In other words, ships are designed for the purpose of ocean sailing; they are designed to withstand stormy seas and to navigate in unfamiliar waters, especially with a skilled and willing skipper at the helm. Staying safe in harbor defeats the purpose of having a skipper and, for that matter, owning a ship. And yet just because the skipper has a ship that is capable doesn't mean he or she pulls out of port on some false sense of bravado because he or she has a steel, seaworthy ship. A good skipper constantly evaluates the weather, the tides, the ocean traffic, and the season as well as the cargo and crew on board; he or she is not afraid to ask the right questions, the tough questions, and is always evaluating the facts and questioning potential outcomes in order to secure the right route to get to the ultimate destination. The lack of information on any one of these elements raises the level of risk exponentially and makes determining the right course of action more difficult. A good and responsible skipper will not sail out on a gut feeling that the ship can make the journey. Such blind risks make for good movie scenes but more than likely will have a disastrous impact on the ship and crew.

During my tenure as a street agent in Los Angeles, I received a call regarding the seizure of a load of cocaine in a vehicle that came across the US-Mexico border. The officer on the phone was talking very fast, stating that the driver of the vehicle containing several hundred pounds of cocaine had agreed to cooperate and they (law enforcement officers) were currently driving to East Los Angeles to deliver the vehicle to some waiting bad guys. As I attempted to slow the conversation down, I was met with a flurry of excitable statements by the officer, who was declaring that this was the largest amount of cocaine their agency had ever seen and that they were under a short time frame and would never get the chance to deliver the load if they didn't take fast action. I began to ask a series of questions, such as: What do we know about the bad guys? What do we know about the cooperator? Do you have any phone numbers? Do you believe the cooperator? Do you have air support? Can we replace the drugs with counterfeit stuff? Can the vehicle be disabled? Almost all the questions were met with "No. We don't know; that's not important right now!" I strongly advised the officer to slow the operation down until we could get a better idea of the who, what, where, and when of the bad guys in order to decide on the right course of action. Again, I was told, "We don't have time. This is really big, and we are meeting in a large mall parking lot within the hour!"

When my partner and I arrived at the parking lot, we were met by one of the officers on surveillance. The officer advised that the cooperating defendant stated that he had done three other deliveries like this in the past. The cooperator also told them that when he arrived at the parking lot, he waited to get a coded message from the bad guys and they took the car from him. The plan was to have the cooperator park the car loaded with drugs in the middle of a crowded parking lot and wait at the mall entrance with the keys. When the bad guys showed up to get the keys, they would be arrested. My partner and I looked at each other skeptically. We advised the officer that he just did not have enough information and he should consider shutting down the operation, which he scoffed at.

Like clockwork, the cooperating defendant, accompanied by an undercover officer as a passenger, arrived at the mall parking lot and parked the load vehicle in the center of the busy lot. The cooperating defendant then walked to the front of the mall entrance and began to wait. Within an hour, the cooperator received a call from the bad guys indicating that they were on the way to the location. Since the parking lot was extremely busy with vehicles, part of the plan was to concentrate surveillance on the cooperator, keeping undercover officers close by to affect the arrest when he turned over the keys. After about an hour, a voice coming over the radio cried out, "Where the hell is the load car?" This was followed by a number of calls stating, "The car is gone! The car is gone!" Officers darted throughout the parking lot searching frantically for the vehicle while other officers took off in opposite directions to see if they could locate the load car on the highway. The cooperating defendant was whisked away to another location where officers began to interrogate him, as they now believed he had had something to do with the missing load vehicle. Over and over again, the cooperating defendant adamantly stated that this was exactly what had happened in previous deliveries.

The video footage of the parking lot was subsequently reviewed and revealed that at approximately the same time the cooperator received a call from the bad guys, two unidentified male suspects simply walked up to the load vehicle with a set of keys, opened the vehicle, and drove out of the parking lot without any hesitation. The vehicle had been gone for over forty-five minutes before anyone knew it was missing. Faced with the surveillance footage, the officers now began to refocus their questions more specifically to the cooperating defendant. What they learned was that the cooperator had never lied to them; the officers just didn't ask the right questions and made a number of incorrect assumptions on how the delivery would take place. The officers would learn that the cooperator did routinely deliver the load vehicle to the parking lot and then receive a coded message when the traffickers were on their way to pick up the load car. The officers assumed the driver had to hand the keys over to the traffickers so they never asked questions beyond what happened at the mall. The cooperator said he was initially instructed to always take the keys with him and to wait in the mall. After about an hour, he would receive another coded message to tell him to take a bus back to the border and would be paid within a couple of days. He used the same vehicle each time and used the same keys each time. The traffickers minimized their exposure to the cooperator by having a separate set of keys and utilizing coded messages to identify their locations and their identities.

Because the cooperator had stated that he always had to be at the mall by a specific time, the officers let a sense of urgency, coupled with the fact that this was such a large load of drugs, override their operational and tactical sense, resulting in the loss of a significant amount of cocaine as well as a dead end in discovering the full identity of the trafficking group. They did not evaluate all the pieces of information or the lack of information to come up with a prudent and responsible risk analysis that would leverage and guide the correct course of action for a successful enforcement plan. Had they evaluated all the information, had they asked the right questions, they would have instituted a number of operational precautions to minimize the risk of the loss of drugs and the identity and apprehension of the suspects. Instead, they let their bravado and the potential glory of future success cloud their judgment, which ultimately sank their seaworthy ship!

CHAPTER 8

STEWARDSHIP

THERE IS IN THE COURSE of a career or a lifetime a defining moment that so impacts you or your organization that you are forever changed. That moment, no matter how brief, has a way of changing how you view the world and in many cases how you view yourself. It can be a moment or even a season that defines your purpose and calling with great clarity.

On the morning of September 11, 2001, I was accompanying DEA's chief of operations to a meeting with the intelligence staff in the east building of DEA headquarters. Following the meeting, as we walked through the lobby, I noticed a crowd of employees gathered around the television set. We were told that a plane had just hit one of the towers of the World Trade Center in New York City. By the time we arrived at our office on the twelfth floor of the west building, it was clear that the United States was under attack. As we watched the Twin Towers erupt with horrific flame and destruction on television, the office was noticeably silent. We watched the surreal scene with disbelief for several minutes, until the silence was broken by the voice of Larry Gallina exclaiming, "What the hell is that?" Larry pointed to an American Airlines jet that was completely out of the pattern, in a nose-down angle of attack heading directly toward the Pentagon. We could hear the engines screaming as American Airlines Flight #77 disappeared into the west side of the Pentagon at over five hundred miles per hour followed by the explosion that rocked our building. We immediately evacuated the building, fearing that we would be hit next.

At the rallying point at ground level, I was surrounded by some of the most decorated and seasoned drug enforcement agents in the world. Many, if not all, of us had spent our entire adult lives as risk-aggressive individuals, who daily took the fight to drug traffickers throughout the streets in this country as well as in the international arena. Now all we could do was look at each other with vacuous eyes, trying to figure out what to do next. We knew what to do on the street against drug traffickers. We knew instinctively how to react to the sound of gunfire, but this was different. We were under attack. Planes were crashing out of the skies into buildings. What next? Car bombs? Snipers? Chemicals? It was the roar of an F-16 overhead that finally moved us to action in securing the perimeter of the building after which we initiated our plan to ensure our continuity of operations as an executive branch of the government.

In the coming year, I witnessed the almost miraculous renovation of the Pentagon. As the newly appointed chief of domestic operations for DEA, my office directly overlooked the Pentagon, and I was able to daily observe the progress that was made. As the one-year anniversary of 9/11 approached, I found myself becoming more uneasy and uncomfortable each time looking at the Pentagon building and reminiscing about the events of that tragic day. On the day of the anniversary, I was scheduled to give a speech in Denver, Colorado, for my good friend and former partner Jeff Sweetin. Jeff had been recently promoted to the special agent in charge of the Rocky Mountain Field Division and had asked me to come out to speak to his division on leadership. A week before my speech, I called Jeff and explained that I felt it was necessary to stay in DC during that time. As I spoke to Jeff, I revealed to him that I was wrestling with feelings of guilt for not being here on the anniversary and that, more important, I had been feeling like I should have done more the morning of 9/11. Jeff was gracious and understood. He confided that he too had been dealing with the same issues.

After hanging up the phone, I went up to my bedroom and began to wrestle with thoughts that I should have done more that day. I found myself quietly agonizing over an overwhelming sense of guilt that came over me. My wife came into the room, and I tried to hide my face from her as she asked what was wrong. All I could say was that I should have done more. I should have gone to the Pentagon. We were safe while others were dying and needed our help ... *I* should have done more ... *We* should have done more. Over the course of the following year, I had the opportunity to meet several individuals in public service who were dealing with the same issues.

This is the heart of the warrior; this is the true calling of the public servant—wanting, willing, and needing to help others they will never know! They are men and women who are more than willing to leave everything behind, including family, friends, and safety, to ensure that others will live. We find it almost impossible not to go toward the sound of gunfire, toward the sounds of chaos, toward the cries for help! We have to. We are wired that way. Warriors long to have been on the planes that got hijacked because we know we would have saved them all. That's what makes ours different from other professions, because deep down, a true warrior understands and recognizes that love requires action and sacrifice. And when warriors can't act, when they are prevented from acting, or when they fail to act, they can become forever wounded inside.

That season following the attacks of 9/11 redefined for me who I was and what my purpose and calling was as a leader in public service. Although I understood that there was evil in the world, the events of

9/11 made this evil tangible. It was radical and blinding and sought to destroy and enslave free people. I began to fully appreciate that this evil threat in the world spanned far beyond drug-trafficking organizations. You see, I always understood that the drug traffickers were in business because they profited on the backs of the addicted and they stayed in this business in order to live an obscene and opulent lifestyle far from the reach of American justice. But now I understood that there were people and organizations that truly hated us, America, as a people—they hated our way of life, they hated our system of justice, they hated our regard for individual civil rights and liberty, and most of all, they hated our collective and individual freedoms we enjoy and protect. These same individuals and organizations would stop at nothing to partner with drug-trafficking groups in order to finance their terror operations in an attempt to destroy us and our way of life. As the reality of this set in over the course of a season, so did the understanding that I really only had a moment to make a difference, that part of my responsibility as a leader was to ensure that I was a good steward with the time that I had left in my profession.

You have to understand what a steward really is. You see, a steward holds something in place for another; it's that simple. As leaders in any organization, we have a brief window of opportunity to make a difference in the lives of those who are entrusted to us. In fact, I believe that as leaders, we have a moral obligation to make things better—not perfect. We have to do our best in the time we have to ensure that we leave our positions and our organizations a little better than they were when they were given to us. As leaders, we must understand that everything we have is just temporary and we should be asking ourselves, "What will I do with the time and opportunity that has been given to me?" You may think of stewardship in terms of making an investment. Any time you invest in something—whether the stock market or a purchase of any sort—there is always a risk involved in what the return on that investment will be. Some leaders base their investments in an organization on what *they* will receive as a beneficiary first and the organization second or not at all. This is nothing more than a corrupt leader who will ultimately doom the organization, as was discussed in earlier chapters. There are also leaders who will not invest in their people or organization because they just don't have the time; they are lazy leaders who will miss out on reaping any organizational benefit. But then there are those leaders who willingly step out and demonstrate courage, who take the time and the risk to invest in the lives of their people, knowing full well the danger involved. What risk? Didn't we just talk about that? Yes, we did, but the risk in investing in people is that some of our people won't get it and some are just not interested in being invested in (shoe salesmen), but those that do and are, they will make a difference and given the opportunity will continue to make a positive change in any organization. Often when I speak about stewardship and the benefit of investing in the lives of others, I share the story of the parable of talents:

For it will be like a man going on a journey, who called his servants and entrusted to them his property. To one he gave five talents, to another two, to another one, to each according to his ability. Then he went away. He who had received the five talents went at once and traded with them, and he made five talents more. So also he who had the two talents made two talents more. But he who had received the one talent went and dug in the ground and hid his master's money. Now after a long time the master of those servants came and settled accounts with them. And he who had received the five talents came forward, bringing five talents more, saying, "Master, you delivered to me five talents; here I have made five talents more." His master said to him, "Well done, good and faithful servant. You have been faithful over a little; I will set you over much. Enter into the joy of your master." And he also who had the two talents came forward, saying, "Master, you delivered to me two talents; here I have made two talents more." His master said to him, "Well done, good and faithful servant. You have been faithful over a little; I will set you over much. Enter into the joy of your master." He also who had received the one talent came forward, saying, "Master, I knew you to be a hard man, reaping where you did not sow, and gathering where you scattered no seed, so I was afraid, and I went and hid your talent in the ground. Here you have what is yours." But his master answered him, "You wicked and slothful servant! You knew that I reap where I have not sown and gather where I scattered no seed? Then you ought to have invested my money with the bankers, and at my coming I should have received what was my own with interest. So take the talent from him and give it to him who has the ten talents."[26]

I know, I know; it is sort of heavy, but it does make a really good point about being a good steward. Let me point out a few things in the parable that are often missed. First, the owner of the goods, the man, understands that each of the three servants has varying degrees of abilities: *"And to one he gave five talents, to another two, and to another one, to each according to his own ability."* The story also declares that the man is going on a journey, so it is expected that he will be gone for a long time; again, clearly the man did not expect the money (talents) he gave them to be just held but for them to be good stewards with the money and to use it in a fruitful way and according to their respective ability. The first two servants did and doubled their money, but when it came to the last, he declared he was fearful of the man and in his mind, it was better to just hold on to the money than to risk losing it. The man implies that the servant knew he would have at least earned interest on the money if he placed it in a bank, but the servant did nothing and his unwillingness to act is described as wicked and lazy.

Here is what I find interesting in the parable: the man never declared that the servants had to be successful with the money. He did expect them to act in accordance with their ability. Even of the servant that he gave the one talent to he fully expected some type of action. I often have thought that if the servant used the one talent to buy a grapevine and the vine died, the man would have said, "Hey, at least you tried." But he did nothing; he was too lazy even to invest it in a bank. This is what happens when leaders become fearful and lazy and fail to make investments in the lives of their personnel. After a while, it's easier not to make any investment at all, which will cause any group, section, or organization to stagnate. Never let fear steer; be willing to step out and make an investment in the lives of others. I recognize that's harder than it sounds, and sometimes a leader must be willing to put it all on the line. I read a great line on a LinkedIn site that went like this: "COO to CEO: 'What if we invest in our people and they leave?' CEO to COO: 'What if we don't and they stay?'"[27]

CHAPTER 9

WORK-LIFE BALANCE

L ET ME ASK YOU A couple of questions: what is the secret to success, and what do you consider is a waste of time? These seem like opposing questions, but really, when you give it some thought, they complement each other. I often have had the great honor of speaking to a group of young students who belong to the Fellowship of Christian Athletes. The ages range from somewhere in middle school all the way up to high school seniors. I almost always start out by making the declaration: "You are all destined for greatness!" The problem is many young people have a twisted sense of what greatness truly means, and this can be carried into adulthood.

Unfortunately, we all know individuals who made it to the top, to "greatness," by scratching and clawing their way up through an organization only to look back and see a wake of destruction they have left behind. Even more disturbing is that there are those who justify to themselves that this is the life one needs to pursue if he or she is going to make it to the top. In other words, I had to step on people; I had to leave my wife or husband; I had to spend more time at work than at home; I had to leave my children; I had to leave my faith; I had to ...! Yet we all instinctively realize that if we are given the opportunity to be alert while we are drawing our last few breaths of life, none of us will be saying, "I wish I had one more hour in the office; I wish I could make one more dollar, score one more contract, receive one more award! Instead, even the most balanced people tend to have regrets about what a life spent truly means in terms of significance.

I am in no way suggesting that leaders should not work hard and be driven toward excellence, as there is nothing worse than mediocrity, which is the enemy of excellence. I am saying that we all need to recognize when we are getting out of balance. When your career, your profession, your calling in life begins to overpower you, it may be time to step back, reevaluate, and redefine what your priorities and your purpose truly should be.

I pulled into my driveway at about 10:30 p.m. on Friday night after finishing another sixteen-hour day in headquarters. This had become the routine for me since my appointment as the chief of domestic operations. I sat there for a moment thinking about how each day was becoming increasingly more frustrating and demanding and there no longer was any sense of fun or for that matter accomplishment, just one fire drill after another. I kept a pretty good front up at work, but by the time I got home, I was miserable, almost dreading the sound of the alarm clock that would come at 4:15 a.m. But this was Friday evening, I was relieved that I could at least sleep in tomorrow until my six kids got up in the morning and started running around. As soon as I entered the house, I quickly got changed into some jeans and warm clothing, poured myself a large cocktail, and went out onto my back deck. While staring out into the darkness, trying to decompress from the events of that week, I heard the sliding glass door open and close behind me. It was my wife, Shelly. She tapped me on the shoulder and quietly stated, "I need to talk to you." As I turned around and looked into the eyes of the beautiful woman staring up at me, she simply said, "The kids are worried about you. I am worried about you. You are aging in front of us."

I stood there momentarily taking in what she had just said; I wasn't shocked or remotely surprised because she was right and I knew it. I held on to her for a long time, and after letting go, I looked at her and just said, "Okay."

When Monday morning came, I called my deputy assistant Matt into my office and told him that I was done. Matt looked at me inquisitively, and I went on to say, "Matt, that's it; we are going to start shutting down here at six, and we are going to do our best to get out of here no later than six thirty; I am done with the sixteen- to eighteen-hour days. My family thinks I am coming apart, and to be honest, I sometimes feel the same way." Matt smiled and said that was good with him. "I am probably going to piss off the bosses, but I will deal with that!"

Crazy as this sounds, our headquarters personnel were so used to working these types of hours that when people left at five or five thirty, they actually felt a little guilty. In fact, I was present when a senior executive chided others about leaving "early" at five thirty, even though they worked a twelve-hour day! We had become our own worst enemy and started to believe this tempo was the norm. It's not. It's bad, and it makes for a significantly unbalanced workforce! In fact, when I look back at that time frame, I have to laugh a little because my neighbors thought for a long time that my wife was a single mom with six kids and that I was the boyfriend who visited on weekends! More important, I began to realize that I had more patience with the people at work than I had with my own family (something I continue to work on).

It was not easy to attempt to break this habit, as I often worried about the perception of leaving early (again, early meant a twelve- to fourteen-hour day while in DC), but I consistently attempted to close up our shop by either six or seven at night. Once I made the decision to become a little more balanced, I began to notice a strain between me and my immediate superior, as there were several times that I received a phone call asking where I was, followed by me stating, "I am on the way home." It took me some time to fully appreciate the amount of time I spent away from home pursuing my calling. While I have always thought I was pretty balanced (up until the night my wife spoke to me), it was our move to Florida that put things in perspective.

While stationed in Florida, my wife and I were blessed to make friends with a number of families in our neighborhood. This was the first time in my career that we actually had close friends who were not in the law enforcement profession. They were always interested in how my wife managed to juggle six kids and move around the country. On a number of occasions, while talking about events with the children, I heard my wife say, "Well, Jim wasn't around that much during this time." About the third or fourth time I heard her say that, I became angry. I pulled her off to the side and asked, "Why do you keep saying I wasn't around much?" My wife looked at me like I was a crazy man, and then, as if I had told one of the best jokes ever heard, she started to laugh—not a ha-ha laugh but a gut-wrenching belly laugh. No kidding! When she composed herself, she put her hand on my shoulder and said, "Ahh, honey, you are a great dad and a great husband, but really, you were away from home ... a lot. It's okay; you love your job, and I always knew this was your calling. Besides, it's not as bad anymore, and we love you!" Wow, not as bad anymore ... How bad was it then? I am blessed beyond what I deserve to be married to the kind of woman men dream of and am equally blessed that my children, all six of them, despite my shortfalls, have grown into men and women of character, integrity, and purpose. But it easily could have gone the other way, and I recognize that.

I have become increasingly critical (it's a spiritual gift) when I read about the experts who give us reasons as to why people in some professions are prone to one social malady, vice, or another. Now, while some professions are in fact more stressful and may have a higher degree of danger, they are typically sought out by those individuals who are attracted to or feel led to pursue that type of work. But because you choose a certain type of work does not necessarily mean that you are suddenly "genetically disposed" to some social malady. Let me further explain. When I was pursuing a career in law enforcement, I would routinely run into people (some cops) who would state, "Oh man, most cops I know are drunks and divorced," as if that was the normal course of your life if you chose a law enforcement path because according to them, that was what happened to people who became cops! The reason for this was, according to simple logic, the profession came with high stress and extreme danger, as well as the requirement of dealing with the dregs of society and so on and so on. And while this is absolutely true, it does not mean that it will lead to the implosion of a law enforcement officer, unless he or she makes the decision to let it take over his or her life and does nothing to mitigate the situation. The same is true for any given profession, if you allow yourself to become unbalanced in pursuit of your career.

I grew up in a cop's home. My father was a New York City police officer and had what we think was only a tenth-grade education. After realizing that I was actually going to pursue this career, my father would always tell me that I had to maintain the right attitude as a police officer. He would tell me that regardless of how good of a cop I became, people—especially those I would serve—would be critical and question my motives because I represented authority. He would say that nobody likes to be told what to do, but as a police officer, part of my duty was just that, which meant that the public would be critical of my job. He would also say that it was so important that I maintain the moral high ground, as I would not be immune to the vices that impacted others. Finally, he told me that he shared everything with my mom, his wife. "I always told

Mom everything, no matter what occurred that day; she knew how my day went. Some guys hid things, but I never did."

I don't want the reader to conclude that somehow I am oversimplifying or dismissing the overwhelming amount of evidence and studies on stress-related incidents in the job market and the factors that are involved. What I am stating is that as leaders we have the responsibility to "manage expectations" with our workforce. We do this by establishing a relationship with our people and stressing the importance of a balanced work life as well as providing them an avenue that will assist them and their families with issues should they arise, such as the employee assistance programs or a chaplain's program as examples.

It took me a while to fully appreciate what my father said about having the right attitude at work. While sitting in a police chief's office, I noticed a devotional he had framed on his wall in the conference room. The devotional was written by very well recognized pastor and speaker, Chuck Swindoll. It said:

> The longer I live, the more I realize the impact of attitude on life. It is more important than the past, than education, than money, than circumstances, than failures, than successes…

> I am convinced that life is 10% what happens to me and 90% how I react to it. And so it is with you … we are in charge of our attitude.[28]

I have started to wrap my arms around the choices I make each day. I have the ability to choose how I respond to a given set of circumstances, so I own how I ultimately decide to respond. I realized my father was right: approaching your job with the right attitude is critical to your success, critical to your well-being, and critical to your work-life balance. So the fact that we have a tendency to spend more time with our work family than our own is not an excuse to fail at life; we need to encourage our people to recognize the importance of a balanced work life so as not to ignore the needs of their families. In the end, it's not our job that makes us get divorced; the job does not make us have affairs, and the job does not make us disregard our responsibility to our children or our respective faiths. We make choices about these issues based on our attitude toward circumstances and then find it convenient to blame work for our collective shortfalls. This is unacceptable, and we need to practice the art of encouragement with our people. They need to understand and appreciate that their leaders want them to succeed both personally and professionally. So as leaders, we need to convey to our people that it is "they" who have to take ownership of their attitude; we can't fix it for them. While any one of us may be dealing with a multitude of personal and professional issues, problems, and circumstances, we (the person in the mirror) are solely responsible for how we deal with them. It is our attitude that ultimately drives our response.

CHAPTER 10

THE TRUTH ABOUT FAILURE

I WAS LISTENING TO THE RADIO the other day when the announcer began to talk briefly about failure. She went on to say oh so very softly that "failure is just success dressed up in a different package so we should celebrate failure when it comes." I thought for a moment of how profound this was and then came to my senses and yelled back at the radio, "What a bunch of crap!" Later that same day, I made the mistake of looking at a number of articles and blogs regarding failure only to find that most of the writings were incredibly sappy, filled with philosophical musings about the significance of failing. Now I realize that for many of the authors, their intention was to point out that we learn from failure and that often adversity builds character. No argument here, but much of what was written about was just, well, sort of nuts! In fact, one blogger even wrote that "Great leaders fail most of the time." Are you kidding me? I don't want to work for any leader who fails nine out of ten times; failure sucks, really. Let's not kid ourselves. I don't know any sane person who celebrates losing a game, a contest, or a marriage and profits during the last quarter or any other endeavor in life! No one likes to fail, unless you are a little off!

In a previous chapter, I described some leaders who are so afraid of failure that they will never move outside of their safe zone. Fear keeps them and their organization from growing, which quite honestly, can lead to failure. Then there are those leaders who refuse to recognize failure under any circumstances. They lie to themselves and to the organization by believing and/or suggesting that success is just around the corner or will come in the next quarter, all the while sinking and becoming further trapped in their self-imposed quicksand. Failure should never be an option for anything or anyone. However, the fact is that failure does happen and is, for the most part, inevitable in life's journey. So what if our section, team, or organization is failing or beginning to fail? How do we as leaders respond to failure? How do we initiate the change necessary to alter the course toward success, to mitigate failing?

There is a marriage principle that is taught by counselors to spouses who have failing relationships; they are to say, "I love you," even though they may despise their spouse; "I love you" even though they may hate their spouse; "I love you, and I care about you; you are important to me!" This is taught in order to speak life back into a relationship, and the fact is that often, our words are evidence of what we have in our heart. Therefore, you may soon find that your heart will follow your words.

For leaders who have organizational challenges, we need to be willing to speak about our core values and what they mean and mean what we say about the importance of organizational health and the significance of our people. As I have said, words have meaning, so I think it is necessary to define the meaning of *failure*:

1. A person or thing that is unsuccessful or disappointing;
2. the cessation of normal operations;
3. a decline or loss;
4. the fact of not reaching the required standard; or, my favorite,
5. "nonperformance of something required or "expected"[29]

Nothing in any of these definitions describes it as a finality, and the fact is that a person, organization, or team must be willing to face failure when it happens and find the courage and tenacity to overcome it and learn from the circumstances that caused the failure. Therefore, as leaders, we don't plan for failure; rather, we are constantly striving to mitigate the risk of failure. Successful leaders accomplish this by developing and articulating a *vision* for their organization and people and demonstrating *faith, courage,* and *perseverance* in pursuit of that vision.

Once again, words have meaning, and according to the dictionary, the word *vision* is a noun defined as the *act or power of anticipating that which will or may come to be.*[30] In *The Power of Leadership,* John Maxwell briefly describes how so many people live reactive lives based on what happens to them rather than proactive lives. They live their lives by accident rather than on purpose.[31] I often ask my audience if they have a vision for their personal and professional lives. I am surprised by the number of blank stares I receive. Living a *proactive* life requires that the individual have a plan. In order for an organization to thrive, there must be a plan, a vision, a purpose to exist. There is a Jewish proverb that states: "Without vision the people perish."[32] This type of "vision" is best described as a blueprint. Again, I submit that leaders who pursue excellence have the ability to articulate the organization's blueprint.

A very close friend of mine, whom I had not seen since our DEA Academy days, met me for lunch at my residence during my headquarters tour. As we reminisced about our days in training, I began to discuss how I was doing my best to plan for the future both for my family and my profession. I told him how I had come to sense how temporary my time here at this assignment was, and I went on discussing how my wife and I were doing our best to plan out some future goals. In the course of speaking to him, midsentence, I realized that he was staring at me with his mouth somewhat open. I stopped short of the next sentence to ask what was wrong. He paused for a few seconds and then said quite softly, "I have never thought about any of that stuff; I really never planned much of anything. I need to start hanging out with you more!" You see, my friend was going through life quite accidentally, like the song "Que Sera Sera"—whatever will be, will be!" If you are on a journey with no map or no direction, how will you know if or when you arrive at your destination? The same is true for organizational leaders. What is your blueprint, your plan? How are you articulating this to your people?

Maybe you are not totally convinced about the importance of planning or establishing a blueprint for your personal and professional life, because, as you say, that's great, but during the course of a lifetime, bad things happen, things don't always go according to plan, failure happens, so now what? What about the blueprint? What happens to my plan? Well, let's look at this like building your own home. One of the very first things any builder does is to draw up a blueprint of the home. The blueprint is a detailed instruction, room by room, floor by floor— the locations, design, and sizes of the total area that will make up your home. But even if you have never built your own home, it would not be unusual for you to find that the home you live in right now has actually had several blueprints drawn up prior to its completion. Why? Well, just as you said earlier, "stuff happens!" That is, during the course of building the home, suddenly, the builder may have determined that a window or a door or a room can't go where you want it because the structure or design of the house won't support it. It may even be that you determine that you can't come up with the extra money for the increased square footage. Or even better, you realize that you have extra money to put a second floor on the house. All of these reasons require an adjustment to the original blueprints, or sometimes the entire blueprint has to be scrapped and resubmitted! The builder doesn't decide not to build; he or she never stops building but quickly adjusts the plans.

As leaders, we need to approach our journey the same way, we don't plan on failing; rather, we consistently demonstrate that our expectations for our people, our organization, are to pursue excellence and succeed. However, we need to anticipate the possibility that in the course of our planning and during the course of following our blueprints, we may be required to make adjustments. While I can't overemphasize the importance of planning, we should not be consumed by it or the process. There are a number of leaders who are so busy planning for tomorrow that they forget about what they need to do today! They miss out on the opportunities to succeed in the present. Let me offer this piece of advice: don't live in the past, but learn from it; don't live for the future, but plan for it. Live and make a difference today, in the here and now. Ask yourself, as a leader: am I living and walking a proactive life, or am I living my life, my calling, by accident?

Once again, I submit that successful leaders have the ability to pursue excellence and mitigate failure by developing and articulating a *vision* for their organization and people and demonstrating *faith, courage,* and *perseverance* in pursuit of that vision. I have described a vision as a plan or a blueprint to follow, but you need to have faith in your plan as well. I am not talking about blind faith; rather, you as a leader have to acknowledge, agree, and trust that your plan, your blueprint, is accurate. This type of faith lights a fire in your belly that leads to passion and conviction and purpose of action. In order for your people to understand this, as a leader, you have to be willing to communicate and share your passion, your conviction, to articulate not only the organization's purpose but the importance of their purpose to the organization. Once again, this requires you as a leader to establish a relationship of trust with those you serve. So communication is another essential element to the health and growth of any organization.

Still, a great plan combined with a firm trust and agreement of the same are of no value if you lack the physical, moral, or mental courage to execute your plan. In fact, fear of failure is a major impediment and reason why some leaders never reach their intended potential. Developing and implementing an effective organizational plan may require you and/ or the organization to move beyond your "comfort zone." This requires the willingness to change an organizational mind-set, which is often difficult because no one really jumps up and cheers for change. It's like the caveman and fire … "Fire bad. Fire burn. Og no like fire!" This of course is true until Og realizes that fire keeps him warm, cooks his food, and keeps the saber-toothed tiger at bay. "Ahh, fire good!"

Therefore, it is important for leaders to understand that apprehension, fear, or reluctance to move can have a detrimental impact on growth, both in terms of the leader and the organization as a whole. So courage is the ability to be willing to step out and execute your plan, your blueprint, with boldness. In doing so, leaders demonstrate to their people that the pursuit of excellence is more important than organizational comfort. Finally, but in no way the least, perseverance is that steady course of action and belief that despite difficulty, despite obstacles, you will succeed, your organization will succeed, your people will succeed. Perseverance always, always births hope, and while hope in and of itself is never a strategy, it is that palpable sense and expectation that success is achievable. Failure is not an option!

My son Mark is a very dedicated young man, who is committed to pursuing his calling of one day leading men and women in public service. His pursuit of this calling led to him attending a prestigious military academy. For over four years, including one year at a prep school, Mark pushed his way through the academic rigors of academy life. Every day was an academic struggle for him, and the fear of getting thrown out of the academy for academic failure was something he lived with constantly. At the end of his junior year, after receiving his class ring and his ceremonial saber, he called me to let me know he was being assigned to a patrol boat in Santa Barbara for his summer assignment. He said excitedly, "Pop, I am almost there, just one more year!" But just two weeks into his summer assignment, Mark was ordered back to the academy as a result of the recommendation from an academic review board that decided he would be dismissed for failing a physics course. In his appeal to the commandant, Mark wrote:

> I have been told by some that because of my academic weakness that I don't measure up, that I don't belong here, that I am not officer material, but I refused to believe this and I don't believe it now. I am not at all minimizing the fact that academics have not been my strongest attribute, but for the past three years I have proven time and time again that walking away or resigning was never an option for me. I truly believe that I am called to serve as a warrior no matter how hard or how long it takes … I recognize the precarious situation I am in and I am troubled and afraid, but giving up is just not in my nature. I cannot nor will not promise that if given the opportunity that I will suddenly become an A student. What I can promise is that Mark Capra will never give up, I will endeavor to endure, to drive forward.[33]

After almost three months of waiting, Mark received the news that his appeal was denied. He was crushed emotionally and in spirit. As he was walked back to his dorm to pack out, he was escorted by a senior noncommissioned officer who did his best to encourage him to pursue his dream. Pushing through the emotional pain of rejection and failure, Mark simply declared, "I was raised a champion, and I will get back up!" Throughout this challenging season, he has consistently demonstrated a willingness to pursue his vision with courage, commitment, and tenacity. He is now finishing his college degree and expects to attend officer candidate school within a year in order to pursue his calling as a leader. Mark is destined for greatness, and while he would be the first one to say that failure really sucks, that it is painful and can be demoralizing, and if you let it, it can overpower you, he would also declare that failure is not and never can be an option.

CHAPTER 11

WHAT WILL BE YOUR LEGACY

AVE YOU EVER REALLY CONSIDERED why you are here? Really, why have you been put on this earth? In previous chapters, I wrote about that moment of clarity when, for whatever the reason, you begin to understand that we only have a moment here. Once you begin to wrap your mind around this, the next question should be: what will I do with the brief time that is allotted to me?" My good friend and fellow leader Dan Salter often quotes his "posturepedic theology."[34] Dan asks his people, "When you are on your deathbed, who will be at your bedside and why?" So now I will ask, have you considered what your legacy will be? I mean, if you died today, what would be your legacy at your home and at work? There is a Jewish proverb that states, "Life is like a vapor, a mist, here for a moment, then suddenly gone."[35] Pericles, the fifth-century BC leader of Athens said, "What you leave behind is not what is engraved on stone monuments but what is woven into the lives of others."[36]

My son Doug is a young US Marine officer who has served two tours in Afghanistan. During his tours in theater, I would routinely send him a message that would simply say, "Hope you are well. I am proud of you. Love and take care of your marines." During his first tour, I received a message from him that startled me: "Dad, the one thing I have really learned here is what bad leadership looks like!" The note went on to describe a particular commander who was by all accounts a very poor leader. I just stared at the screen for a long time trying to figure out how to respond while thinking about the real ramifications of bad leadership in a combat zone. I started out by responding:

> Son, never forget what bad leadership looked like, what it felt like, and how it impacted you and your marines. Men and women thirst and hunger for good leadership. They instinctively know what it looks like, how it feels; the very air around a good leader is palpable. Shield your marines the best that you can from bad leaders and the legacy they leave in the hearts of men; love them, care for them, be accountable to them, and make sure that they are accountable to you. Sometimes you learn more from a bad leader than a good leader. At times we take a very good leader for granted, and we assume he or she will just make the right decisions. When hell rains down on your team, they will look to the good leader, the right leader, and that has to be you; they will look to you for direction, guidance, and courage in the face of chaos, and they will follow. Never forget you chose to lead, you chose to love them, you chose to enter the arena; seize this moment to train them up. Let them help you become a better leader. Doug, the funny thing about this leadership journey is that we never truly arrive; we just continue to lead and learn. Always strive to make a positive difference in the lives of the men and women who are entrusted to you.

Stay strong, stay focused. I love you and continue to be very proud of you. Semper Fi, Pops

By the time I pushed the send button, I was weeping partly because of the fact I know my son, the man and leader he has become, but mostly because I have become part girl in my older age. But it is true that sometimes we take for granted the really good leaders who come our way. We sometimes do take them for granted because we know that they will make the right decision, but inevitably, the underlying common thread of all great leaders is that they truly care for the men and women they are entrusted to lead.

I didn't know the chief, but I attended his retirement in August of 2007 in order to thank him for his support and partnership with our DEA division. The chief was a career public servant and had served twenty-seven years with a small North Texas Police Department. He was one of the longest-serving police chiefs in Texas history. The retirement ceremony took place in the civic center building, and as I mingled, I met the usual local dignitaries who attended events such as this. I unfortunately expected the typical mundane retirement ceremony that would come with several hollow accolades from guests and the usual good-bye speech. I could not have been more wrong.

The mayor presided over the ceremony and immediately called on the chief to come up to the podium where he presented him with his badge. During his brief speech, the mayor often spoke of the chief's leadership, which was responsible for building the police department into one of the finest in North Texas. As I looked out toward the guests, I noticed that their eyes were not on the speaker but on the chief. The small crowd looked on with reverence at the chief and delighted in nodding every time an accolade was given to him. What was more striking to me was the mood of his command staff, officers, and professional staff. As each departmental representative stood up to say something, his or her speech was often broken up with tears and raw emotion. Large, hulking Texas lawmen attempted to read the poetic phrases on inscriptions, stopping to wipe away tears and pausing to compose themselves before going on. It became very apparent that his department respected and revered the chief, but they also loved him, not only as their leader, but as a man and a friend. After each presentation, the chief would hug the individual the way a loved one hugs a family member. Throughout the ceremony, the chief was very emotional, and I could often see him shaking his head no when he received recognition regarding his ability and leadership.

Following all the presentations, the chief was asked to speak to the gathering. Wiping tears from his eyes, he began by saying, "I did nothing; it was you all who made this department what it is. I just asked you to do it … and you did." The chief went on to say, "I hope I have been a good leader … and I know I leave this department in great hands …" During that ceremony, I witnessed a snapshot of the life and impact of a true servant leader. Even in the last moments of his retirement ceremony, the chief made sure that it was never about him but emphasized that others were more deserving of the credit for the department's success.

Too often as we walk our leadership journey, we mistakenly look for examples from the grand icons of leadership. We buy their books in search of some new truths that may enlighten and help us along our way. Sometimes, we need only to look in our backyard communities, to people like the chief, who probably never wrote a book on leadership but daily practiced their calling and walked their walk such that they left an indelible legacy behind. The chief's legacy is one that defines the servant leader—a man of servitude, integrity, empathy, commitment, loyalty, and least not, one of love for the men and women of the small police department and the community he served for twenty-seven years.

So what are you weaving into the lives of those you serve, those you are entrusted to lead at home and at work? I know several people who still live with the ghosts of leaders from the past—leaders, both men and women, who were so incredibly self-centered, and egotistical and so often made a sport out of emasculating and intimidating others, that even long after they are gone, when they are spoken about, some people get emotionally ill because they remain angry and bitter about how they and others were treated.

For several years, I remained extremely angry toward a former boss I had worked for, and often when I spoke about his tenure, I found myself reliving my anger toward him. He was a very talented professional but a very moody person. He always seemed to be angry no matter what the topic was, and he was quick to yell and scream and then walk out of a room, leaving those remaining bewildered. On one particular occasion, I was on a conference call with him when all at once he began to yell and accuse me of not caring and being incompetent, and then he hung up the phone on me. My immediate juvenile reaction was to tell him to eat crap and bark at the moon, but since he was no longer on the line, I held my tongue and made an immediate appointment to speak with him.

When we met, deep down inside, I would have liked to immediately initiate what my good friend Rob Brisolari describes as "schoolyard rules"—in other words, start a physical fight for calling me names and making accusations, but again, that's sort of frowned on in government circles and usually not a prescribed course of action in any leadership book. After I told him that I was concerned about his outburst of anger and that it was misplaced, he gave me some excuse that his outburst really wasn't meant for me but for others on the phone. His phony justification only increased my resentment toward him, and I soon found myself doing anything I could to avoid him until I was finally transferred to another division.

I have often cited this experience when speaking on leadership and would go into detail about how he treated his people and what his actions did to alienate those around him. What I noticed was that every time I spoke about this particular experience, I relived the anger and the resentment I had toward him because I had become bitter and not allowed myself to let go. I knew inside that I actually needed to forgive him and move on, but honestly, reliving the experience and anger and pointing out his shortfalls was becoming my way of beating him up in a public venue. (Not a very mature thing to do!) I began to deal with this issue after listening to my pastor speak on forgiveness and letting go offenses that we tend to carry.

You see, being offended can often lead to bitterness, and being bitter will take you where you don't want to go. It's really not the act of being offended that leads to problems; it is the willingness to maintain a tight hold of the offense that impacts you. I have spoken a great deal about loving your people and what love is, but part of truly loving is being willing to let go of an offense; when we don't—or better yet, when we *refuse*—bitterness finds a way to creep in and take a hold of the heart. By not letting go of the offense, I find myself living in the past. If I am living in the past, how can I grow and move toward my future? What I learned is that the whole act of forgiveness is not a feeling that somehow comes over you; just like love, it is a conscious act of the will! So I have to be willing to let go, be willing to release the offense. How am I doing? I'm still working on it. I refuse to let a negative legacy take hold of my heart, but I still have to remind myself to let go; I am not as bad as I was when talking about this experience, but I still have a way to go. I am getting there! I'm getting there!

I am now in the winter of my career and am planning on closing out on my calling to public service this year. I have had the distinct honor and privilege of leading some of the bravest and most talented, dedicated, and committed employees in service to this great nation of ours. I have made a host of mistakes during my leadership journey, but I have been blessed to have been forgiven on a number of occasions by those men and women who really know my heart—and this includes my family. The men and women I have had the honor of serving with have helped me on my journey; they have trained me and guided me, and most of all, they have loved me and my family as their own. I owe a great debt of gratitude to them all and will continue to do everything in my power to pay it forward. I look forward to continuing my leadership journey in my next career wherever the good Lord leads. I am hopeful that the reader enjoyed my journey and that maybe, just maybe, my experience validates something in your heart regarding true leadership. May your own journey be as fruitful and as fun as mine has been.

—Jimmy

ENDNOTES

1. Dave Grossman, *On Killing: The Psychological Cost of Learning to Kill in War and Society* (Little Brown and Company, 2009).

2. *Audit of Department of Justice Conference Planning and Food and Beverage Cost*, United States Office of Inspector General Audit Report 11–43, revised issue October 2011.

3. John Maxwell, *The Power of Leadership* (David C. Cook, January 2001), 16.

4. Dictionary.com, s.v., "Discipline."

5. Robert Vernon, "Why Excellence Is Better than Success," *Law Officer Magazine* (June 2010).

6. Rod Olson, DEA Leadership Conference (Dallas, Texas, 2009).

7. Kent Keith, *Servant Leadership in the Boardroom: Fulfilling the Public Trust* (Greenleaf Center for Servant Leadership, 2008), 7.

8. Rod Olson, DEA Leadership Conference (Dallas, Texas, 2009).

9. Luke 10:25–29, New American Standard Bible.

10. Tom Landry, as quoted by Rod Olson (Dallas, Texas, 2009).

11. Ken Blanchard, *Learning to Lead.*

12. Kent Keith, *Anyway: The Paradoxical Commandments* (1968).

13. Josh McDowell and Bob Hostetler, *Beyond Belief to Conviction* (Tyndale House, 2002).

14. Dictionary.com, s.v., "Morality."

15. Norman Geisler and Frank Turek, *Legislating Morality: Is It Wise? Is It Legal? Is It Possible?* (Bethany House, 1998), 20.

[16] Jim Collins, *How the Mighty Fail and Why Some Companies Never Give In* (Harper Collins, 2009), 55.

[17] Merwyn A. Hayes and Michael D. Comer, *Start with Humility: Lessons from America's Quiet CEOS on How to Build Trust and Inspire Followers* (Greenleaf Center for Servant Leadership, 2010), 17.

[18] Philippians 2:3–5, New American Standard Bible.

[19] Dictionary.com, s.v., "Immoral."

[20] Vincent Cookingham, Lecture on Risk Management, Marist College, May 1985.

[21] John Maxwell, *There's No Such Thing as Business Ethics* (Warner Book), 21.

[22] Ibid., 27.

[23] Dictionary.com, s.v., "Motivate."

[24] John Maxwell, *21 Irrefutable Laws of Leadership* (Thomas Nelson, 1998).

[25] John Maxwell, *The Power of Leadership* (David Cook, 2001).

[26] Matthew 25:14–28, New American Standard Bible.

[27] LinkedIn page (2013).

[28] Chuck Swindoll, *The Importance of Attitude* (2007).

[29] Dictionary.com, s.v., "Failure."

[30] Ibid.

[31] John Maxwell, *The Power of Leadership* (David C. Cook, 2001).

[32] Proverbs 29:18, New American Standard Bible.

[33] Mark Capra, May 2012.

[34] Daniel Salter, Drug Enforcement Administration, Dallas Field Division, Dallas, Texas.

[35] James 4:14, New American Standard.

[36] Quote by Pericles, Greek ruler, 495 BC.

For Speaking Engagements, the author, James L. Capra may
be contacted via LinkedIn or at jlcapra@yahoo.com